Psychotherapy and the Law

Questions and Answers for Counsellors and Therapists

By

PETER JENKINS,
Lecturer in Counselling
Manchester University

VINCENT KETER,
Lawyer
London

JULIE STONE,
Head of Policy and Fitness to Practise
Council for the Regulation of Healthcare Professionals
London

Series Editor
MICHAEL JACOBS

W
WHURR PUBLISHERS
LONDON AND PHILADELPHIA

© 2004 Whurr Publishers Ltd
First published 2004
by Whurr Publishers Ltd
19b Compton Terrace
London N1 2UN England and
325 Chestnut Street, Philadelphia PA 19106 USA

British Library Cataloguing in Publication Data

A catalogue record for this book
is available from the British Library.

ISBN 1 86156 419 8

1004457617 T

Typeset by Adrian McLaughlin, a@microguides.net
Printed and bound in the UK by Athenæum Press Ltd, Gateshead,
Tyne & Wear.

Contents

Chapter 3　　　　　　　　　　　　　　　　　　　　　　**31**

The law in specific contexts

Chapter 4   **50**

Risk and responsibility

Chapter 7   103

Professional activities and the law

Resources   123

Contributors

Peter Jenkins holds qualifications in social work, teaching, management and counselling. He is a lecturer in counselling at Manchester University, a member of the Professional Conduct Committee of the British Association for Counselling and Psychotherapy (BACP), and a BACP-accredited counsellor trainer. He has written widely on the legal aspects of therapy and is the author of *Counselling, Psychotherapy and the Law* (Sage, 1997), co-author with Debbie Daniels of *Therapy with Children* (Sage, 2000), editor of *Legal Issues in Counselling and Psychotherapy* (Sage, 2002) and author of *Exploring Children's Rights* (Pavilion Publishing, 2003).

Vincent Keter holds a law degree from Birkbeck College and is Employment Specialist in the House of Commons Library. He has acted in a number of key legal cases concerning therapists and their professional associations, such as the United Kingdom Council for Psychotherapy and the British Psychological Society. He has represented psychotherapists, counsellors, doctors and clients in disciplinary tribunals, complaints proceedings and judicial review. Vincent has also been involved in consultancy work and is currently completing a PhD in Law and Psychoanalysis at Birkbeck.

Julie Stone (MA, LLB, PGCE), a qualified barrister, has written and lectured on healthcare ethics and law for many years. She is a national and international expert in the field of the regulation, law and ethics of complementary and alternative medicine and has worked closely with the Prince of Wales's Foundation for Integrated Health. She is Head of Policy and Fitness to Practise at the Council for the Regulation of Healthcare Professionals. Her most recent book in this field was *An Ethical Framework for Complementary and Alternative Therapists* (Routledge, 2002).

CHAPTER 1

The law: friend or foe?

Therapists often have a somewhat uneasy relationship with the law. Therapy and the legal system can be seen as being at apparently opposite ends of a spectrum. Whereas therapy is concerned with the client's internal world and is carried on in a private, contained, one-to-one setting, the law ultimately operates in a public arena, open to wider reporting by the media and to intense scrutiny by interested parties. Therapy works with deeply personal material, exploring affect, ambivalence and ambiguity. The law works within apparently clear-cut principles and systems to reach binding decisions about guilt and innocence, liability and compensation.

As therapeutic practice has moved into new arenas, such as primary care, schools and the workplace, it has progressively encountered more and more professional issues with a legal aspect needing to be clarified or resolved. However, unlike comparable professions, such as nursing, teaching and social work, the legal aspects of counselling and psychotherapy have remained a largely underdeveloped element of professional training and practice. This may in part be due to a resistance within the professional culture of therapy towards engagement with what may be seen and experienced as unfamiliar, even hostile, territory. At a more pragmatic level, it may simply be that the widening range of contexts for therapy makes it difficult to provide a legal perspective on practice that shifts in complex ways across private practice, self-employment and volunteer-work settings. While the ethical aspects of counselling and psychotherapy have been the focus of intense and well-justified attention in recent years, the profession has been somewhat slower to engage with the widespread, complex and contradictory kaleidoscope of legal elements to practice. This has, in fact, begun to change in recent years, as professional associations have turned their attention to deal with practitioner concerns for information on key topics, such as confidentiality, data protection and statutory regulation.

Practitioner resistance to engagement with the law can take various forms. For some, the therapeutic relationship provides a clearly boundaried space for work with clients, which needs to exist without any unwelcome intrusion from external interruptions to the frame. It is as if the door to the therapy room can be shut, both literally and metaphorically. The purpose may be to keep client material safely in. The intention may also be to keep out any unhealthy interest in this intensely private therapeutic work by other interested parties, such as child-protection agencies or the Crown Prosecution Service. This perspective is, however, much harder to maintain when the courts show an increasing interest in accessing what were previously seen as the therapist's private and personal reflections on the therapeutic process. For other practitioners, the law seems to hover as an implacable source of authority. It appears to require absolute compliance from practitioners on otherwise complex issues, such as an apparent duty to report child abuse in all circumstances. Considered from a framework drawn from Transactional Analysis (TA), it is as though the law were framed in these instances as a Critical Parent, setting down inflexible rules and expectations, with which the therapist has little option but to comply. Yet, for some practitioners, acknowledging the probable constraints on practice determined by the law can result in adopting a stance of simply refusing to acknowledge or accept legal constraints on professional autonomy. Some therapists doggedly continue to argue that 'second sets of notes' are somehow immune from scrutiny by the courts. Others look for loopholes in data-protection law in order to limit client access. Both groups might provide examples of this kind of Rebel Child attitude towards the law. While these examples are clearly somewhat overdrawn and stereotypical, they do relate to continuing and problematic attitudes towards the law held by some practitioners.

This book aims to encourage and support an alternative approach to the law by therapists, based on a sound and developing knowledge of the basic factors relating to safe, competent and effective therapeutic work. Therapists need to develop their own competence and confidence in using their legal understanding as simply another strand of their professional work. The law and therapy will, it is hoped, work out a relationship based much more on communication and dialogue, grounded in a mutual appreciation of each other's distinct, but complementary, roles.

As suggested above, therapists' attitudes towards the law can be usefully looked at in terms of concepts derived from TA, such as Critical Parent/Adapted Child or Rebel Child. Some practitioner perceptions are based on what are seen as negative features of the law, that is the primacy of logic over emotion, the law's arcane traditions and its overall adversarial approach. The authors' intentions are, therefore, to make information on the law more accessible to practitioners, in a question-and-answer format, and thus promote more of an adult-to-adult dialogue between counsellors and lawyers on the law. It is hoped that a basic grounding in the most important legal principles affecting professional practice will enhance therapists' work and allow them to concentrate on their task of building safe and effective therapeutic relationships.

The terms 'therapist' and 'practitioner' are used here as generic terms to include counsellors, psychotherapists and counselling psychologists. The term 'therapy' similarly relates to forms of psychological intervention, such as counselling, psychotherapy, psychological counselling and psychoanalysis provided on an individual basis.

In order to try and make this book as user-friendly as possible to therapists, a deliberate choice has been made to avoid the heavy use of academic or legal references in the text. This lack of specific detail regarding a particular case or piece of legislation may prove somewhat frustrating for some readers with a more specialist interest in this topic. However, this is perhaps inevitable in trying to produce a book with the widest possible appeal and relevance to practitioners who are looking for a quick and accurate overview of the everyday problems likely to be encountered in their work. Some sources of information, and suggestions for more detailed reading, are included in the Resources section.

CHAPTER 2
Therapy and the law: contracts and liability

This chapter addresses the issue of what the law is and what it consists of. Law is different from ethics, although there are areas of overlap and interplay between the two. The dilemmas facing therapists, such as whether or not to break client confidentiality, will usually have both an ethical aspect and a legal one, and the two may well be in direct conflict. For example, the ethical duty to keep trust with the client may well be perceived by the therapist as being overridden by a legal duty to report serious crime. Resolving these kinds of conflicts is one of the most difficult issues with which practitioners and their supervisors have to grapple. Having a basic knowledge of the legal framework and, perhaps more importantly, how to access more detailed advice as necessary become crucial elements of informed and accountable professional decision-making in this regard.

This chapter introduces basic building blocks of the law, such as tort, contract and statute. Contracts, both with individual clients and with organizations, are looked at. 'Professional negligence', or what therapists can or can't be sued for, is defined. The focus will be on setting practitioner concerns in the overall context of the law and on suggesting guidelines for minimizing the risk of hostile legal action.

As with all the points made in the book, nothing here should be taken as a definitive and unanswerable statement on the law. The law is clearly in a state of flux, and comments offered here may well be rendered outdated by later judgments of the courts or legislation. For every opinion offered here, there will be a credible alternative perspective to be argued by another well-informed legal source. After all, if it really were the case that the law books could provide definite and absolute answers to every question, there would be no need to ever go to court!

The discussion of the law relates mainly to law in England and Wales, as Scotland and Northern Ireland have distinct, and often different, legal systems. Generally, broad legal principles discussed here will also apply to all of the United Kingdom, but the detail, as always, needs to be checked carefully in order to ensure its accuracy.

2.1 How much (or how little) do I need to know about the law as a therapist to avoid problems and to provide a decent service for my clients?

Many therapists seem to be increasingly anxious about the law and are concerned about falling foul of it by accident rather than by design. This is partly because the law is becoming more complex and seems to intrude into counselling and psychotherapy in a great variety of ways. This can include issues such as confidentiality, the use of contracts and data protection, to name just a few areas. Also, the situation in the United States has concerned many practitioners in the United Kingdom, as growing numbers of therapists there have been sued, or have otherwise been involved with the courts, as a result of their practice. This sets a context for current concerns about therapists feeling vulnerable on legal aspects of their work, when this was not, usually, a prominent aspect of any professional training they may have undertaken previously.

Therapists may have had some formal training on the law as part of a prior professional role, for example as a social worker, probation officer or nurse. This will be useful background knowledge to call upon. For others, their previous contact with the law will be limited. It may even be the case that the law is seen as something cold, logical and intimidating – in fact, representing the very opposite of those values that brought therapists to start training and practice in the first place. One of the exercises used in training counsellors about the law often reveals a strong, stereotypical view that lawyers 'earn money out of other people's misfortune'. Of course, this stereotype could just as easily be applied to counsellors and psychotherapists!

Therapists are not lawyers, and the law will probably only ever be a small aspect of therapeutic practice. However, when a practitioner does encounter a problem with a legal dimension, the law, not surprisingly, can become very important in a short space of time. It is worth being aware in advance, therefore, of the kinds of issues that may be worth knowing about. This is both on the grounds of following good (and legally sound) practice and of avoiding major problems in the future wherever possible.

A therapist, as an individual, can choose to know as little as they like about the law. It is worth remembering, however, that professional codes of practice often require that practitioners be aware of the law and seek to work within it as part of good practice. Also, employing agencies, such as colleges, schools, the NHS and voluntary organizations, may well have a requirement to follow particular aspects of the law. Professing complete ignorance of the law might not be seen as indicating good standards of professional practice at a selection interview for a counselling position, for example.

A working knowledge of the law, as applied to practice, needs to cover the basic building blocks with direct relevance to therapeutic work. These areas include:

- **confidentiality**: protecting and disclosing sensitive information
- **data protection**: record-keeping, storing and communicating information
- **contracts**: basic principles of making contracts with clients
- **negligence**: avoiding harm to clients through substandard or exploitative practice
- **discrimination**: complying with the law regarding discrimination on the grounds of race, disability, age, gender and sexual orientation
- **access to legal information and advice**: how to get accurate advice and information on legal issues when needed

Confidentiality is a key concept in counselling and psychotherapy, often flip-charted as part of the ground rules at the very start of any form of training programme. Within therapeutic culture, it may be taken to mean not disclosing the full identity of clients or other trainees in discussing practice issues, without good cause. The law would endorse this approach, as part of the practitioner's 'duty of confidence'. However, few therapists now assume that this duty is *absolute*, although promises of 'completely confidential counselling' may still occasionally be seen on promotional leaflets. There may be an obligation to break confidentiality, that is to disclose client information *without* client consent, in extreme situations, such as threat of harm to self or others, as in the case of suspected child abuse. The state imposes an obligation to pass on information to the authorities in rare situations, such as terrorism and drug-money laundering. Examples of situations where a therapist might consider breaking confidentiality are discussed in more detail elsewhere (see Questions 3.6, 4.2, 4.3, 4.6, 4.7 and 4.8).

Data protection overlaps with confidentiality but has a different basis in law, deriving from specific legislation, that is the Data Protection Act 1998. This sets out the law regarding the records that can be kept on clients, in both computerized and handwritten forms, and outlines the principles of client access to such records. The law here is quite complex. Organizations providing a counselling service need to be fully aware of their legal responsibilities to clients under this Act. In brief, clients have much wider rights now than previously to gain access to records kept on them, whether as written or computerized record, audio- or video-tape. Therapy records now need to be kept with the presumption of possible client access in mind.

Contracts are used by many therapists as part of their work to set out mutual expectations with a client, for the purposes of supervision, or in providing a counselling service to an organization for a fee. The concept of 'contracting' within therapeutic practice provides an overlap of ideas of 'best professional practice' with the law. However, not all contracts for therapy would qualify as a contract in a legal sense, as there are specific conditions for a legal contract to apply. This is particularly important when a therapist is providing a service for a fee, to an individual client or to an employing organization.

Negligence is the term used to describe actions by the therapist that are harmful to the client. This could include abusing the client in financial, emotional or sexual terms, or failing to work to an accepted standard of good practice. The area of law is a branch of law called 'tort' (from the French word for 'wrong') based on medical negligence law. Here, the expectation is that the therapist should work within accepted notions of good practice, as laid down by their particular school or approach. Where the therapist fails to do so and causes the client harm as a result, they may be in breach of their duty of care to the client. This is a type of case heard under civil law, rather than criminal law, and relates to non-intentional harm. Nonetheless, the consequences can be extremely serious for the therapist and for their professional reputation. The harm caused to the client can be either physical or psychological in nature. Psychological harm needs to be sufficiently serious to be classified as a recognized psychiatric condition, such as clinical depression or post-traumatic stress disorder, rather than as simple annoyance or anxiety. This is to prevent the legal floodgates opening, whereby clients could sue whenever they felt hard done by, angry or upset. Restricting claims in this manner also reduces the likelihood of malicious or vexatious litigation.

Therapists need to be aware of the laws which prohibit **discrimination against clients** on the grounds of gender, race, disability or sexual orientation. (Discrimination on the basis of age is currently covered by a voluntary code of practice, rather than by an Act of Parliament, although legislation is now planned on this issue.) Given the strength of values such as acceptance and anti-discriminatory practice within counselling culture, practitioners would, no doubt, want to comply with the law in any event. In reality, the scope of anti-discrimination legislation and the application of the law is often limited to counselling organizations rather than strictly to individual practitioners as such. Therapists would still need to be fully informed about the law as it stands in this area and how it applies in detail to their work.

Finally, therapists cannot be expected to know every aspect of the law relating to their practice. It would be useful, however, to have a good basic grasp of the areas described above. In addition, it is worth knowing how to get hold of more **detailed advice and information** as needed, either to develop a policy as an individual private counselling practice or for a service provider. Details of further sources of such information are provided in the response to 7.7 and in the Resources section.

* * *

2.2 Is a contract for therapy the same as a legal contract or is it something different? What do I need to be aware of in drawing up and using a contract with a client?

A contract for therapeutic work may undoubtedly be a legal contract for the provision of services. However, it could also clearly affect the course of, or have a bearing on, the therapeutic relationship. The word 'contract' has frequently been used to describe the whole range of agreements that can be in place in a therapeutic relationship, covering such matters as agreeing not to self-harm, promising regular attendance at a given time and confirming payment. Not all of these provisions have any legal force.

First, we need to be clear about what a contract is in law. A contract, in the legal sense, is an agreement (oral or written, or both), the terms of which both parties have accepted. Furthermore, it is necessary for a legal contract that both parties intended to be legally bound by their promise when they agreed the terms. For example, a husband's promise to his wife to mend a shelf is not intended to create a legally enforceable agreement by either party. Some of the terms of the therapeutic contract will be intended to create a legal relationship and legal obligations, whereas others will be more directed to the therapeutic relationship. Of course, there will be some overlap.

The other important element of any legal contract is called 'consideration'. This legal term refers to the benefit of the contract to either party. There needs to be consideration for an agreement to be legally binding. Usually, this is the payment that is made by the client for the services. Where the services are given free, there might be some difficulty in finding a legal contract, and probably even greater difficulty in taking legal action based on contract. However, practitioners are still bound by any ethical obligations in any code of ethics under which they are practising and also owe the client a duty of care not to act negligently in their practice.

The second thing to be aware of is that the terms of any agreement can be either *express* or *implied*. 'Express' terms are those terms that are clearly written down or have been clearly communicated verbally. 'Implied' terms are those terms that the court will find to be the valid terms of the contract, even though they have not been written down or verbally agreed between the parties. These fall into three categories:

1. Terms which should be implied because of a 'custom of the trade' to that effect and there is nothing in the contract to contradict them. For example, standards of professional practice that are ubiquitous throughout the profession could be found as implied terms of the contract. The universal ethical prohibition on sexual intimacy in therapy might fall into this category. Accordingly, even if practitioners are not bound by any code of ethics, those professional standards, which have acquired universal acceptance, could become implied terms of any counselling contract.
2. Terms that are implied by statute. Sometimes Acts of Parliament provide for certain circumstances where courts should imply terms into a contract. For example, the Supply of Goods and Services Act 1982 provides for implied terms of 'due skill and care' in the provision of services.
3. Terms that the court will imply because the parties must have intended to include them in order for the contract to be effective. For example, it would probably be an implied term of any contract for therapy that the therapist will provide, or make arrangements to provide, an appropriate venue for the sessions.

It will often be the case that a number of terms in the counselling contract will be present purely to aid the therapeutic relationship and carry no legal force at all. For example, there may be a clause that the therapist will act in the client's best interests at all times. In most cases the professional affiliations of the counsellor or psychotherapist will also form an important aspect of both the legal and professional obligations of the practitioner. In outlining the purely legal aspects, it is important not to lose sight of the non-legal benefits of the contract but also to distinguish clearly the sort of matters that would be relevant in a court of law.

If a written contract is used (which is very much recommended), from a legal point of view, at the very least, it should cover the following areas:

- **Payment**: amount, when payment is due, payment for missed sessions, if payment is linked to a client's resources and, if so, whether there is a duty on the client to disclose the full facts of their financial position.
- **Venue**: practitioner will provide a venue for the therapy, maybe with a reservation of right to change venue (within a limited area). Accordingly, it may be worth including a clause providing that the cost of services may rise if the cost of hiring the venue is increased.
- **Confidentiality**: this should come with a reservation of right to disclose any information to the practitioner's insurer and/or legal advisor

and/or a court of law if necessary, as well as disclosure for the purposes of supervision of clinical practice. Any other limits to confidentiality should be made explicit.

• **Professional Codes**: the contract should disclose the therapist's membership of any professional associations and attach copies of the relevant codes of conduct and complaint procedures that govern the therapy. It may be that not all of the practitioner's affiliations are relevant to the service provided. If the practitioner has more than one professional affiliation, it is probably wise to state which ones are relevant to the therapy in question. Sometimes there are differences between theoretical approaches towards counselling and psychotherapy that may be confusing to the client unless clearly set out.

It is unlikely that any dispute will arise about matters that have been agreed in a clear form. The most important matters of which to be aware are probably the kinds of obligations that might be implied into the contract for counselling by the law in the absence of any written or verbal agreement on that particular point.

The client will not necessarily be in breach of the contract if they do not attend an appointment, but the therapist will probably be in breach for failing to attend. However, if the client fails to turn up to an agreed session, they may still be obliged to pay. If nothing has been agreed about absences, unless the practitioner and client can come to an agreement about a missed session, the question of any obligation of the client to pay will depend on whether there was any implicit agreement to pay for missed sessions – in other words, whether an implied term could be found obliging the client to pay. To avoid argument on this point, it is best to provide for the event of absences and holidays in a written contract.

Section 13 of the Supply of Goods and Services Act 1982 creates an implied obligation of reasonable skill and care in any contract for the supply of services. This could affect a range of issues in the therapy. Poor note-taking by the practitioner, a general lack of attention or any failure to meet accepted standards of ethical practice could all be covered by a statutory implied term of reasonable skill and care. On this basis a client might sue for return of some or all of the fees paid. This is different from the law surrounding negligence, which will probably only become an issue where contractual terms cannot be found, although there is likely to be some overlap between a claim in negligence and a claim for breach of an implied term of reasonable skill and care.

* * *

2.3 I provide analytic psychotherapy for students taking a local diploma in psychotherapy. My problem is that one trainee has had the last year's therapy on account but has now moved away suddenly and is reluctant to pay up. I don't want to resort to legal action, but I do want to be paid for my work!

Non-payment of fees is obviously a breach of contract. Two questions arise. First, who precisely are the parties to the contract and, secondly, what are the possible ways to enforce the contract and obtain payment of the fees?

Most often, the parties to the contract will obviously be the client and the practitioner. However, where services are part of a requirement to complete training, which is very common, the possibility arises of a contract between the therapist and the training institution. This will depend on the particular arrangements in place. For example, if the practitioner is usually paid by the training organization, the obligation to pay for the therapy might lie with the training-course provider. This would probably be more likely if the course charges the student more than the therapist receives and takes an amount, for example, to cover their administration expenses. Of particular importance also would be the question of whether the agreement with the client to defer payment was made by the therapist or by the training course.

If, on the other hand, the practitioner sees the student as a client following on from a referral by the training course, it would be more difficult to claim that the training course is liable to the practitioner for unpaid fees. If the fees are usually paid by the student directly to the practitioner, it would seem very unlikely that the training course would be contractually involved. In each case, the particular facts need to be considered in order to judge whether it is the student or the training course that is obliged to pay the therapist's fees.

There are a variety of approaches to take in recovering fees. Even if litigation is chosen as an option, the court will expect an attempt to be made by the claimant to recover the money owed directly from the client before taking legal action. This usually takes the form of a 'letter before action', where the outstanding sum is requested and the debtor is told that legal action will commence if payment is not made.

If the debtor is clearly not going to pay, legal action may become the only option left to recover the fees. Before taking this step, a number of things need to be considered. The first of these is whether the debtor is simply unable to pay or whether they are unwilling to do so. There is no way of finding this out for sure until after judgment has been obtained and the right arises to question the debtor on their financial position. However, it is usually possible to make an educated guess based on what is already known about the person. It may be the case that the threat of a letter of complaint to the student's professional association, or to their prospective regulatory body, might well have a salutary effect in speeding up payment, though this cannot be guaranteed.

Secondly, depending on the amount of the claim, it may be possible to pursue matters through the small claims track of the civil court system. The small claims limit at the time of writing is £5,000, but that may go up in the future. There are a number of advantages in bringing a small claim. It is often easier to bring the claim without having to employ the services of a lawyer. There are also limited costs consequences to the practitioner, if the claim is lost. In any civil action, the loser usually pays the legal and other costs of the winner. In the small claims jurisdiction, there is no liability to pay the legal costs of the other side, unless the court judges the conduct of either party to be unreasonable, such as taking or defending a claim and then failing to turn up for the hearing without reasonable excuse. This is not to say that costs are not recoverable by the winning party in the small claims court. The court fee (usually small) and any expenses or losses in attending the hearing (including witnesses) are often awarded.

Another important factor to bear in mind is the defendant's home address. If the claim is for a fixed amount (such as unpaid fees – referred to as 'liquidated'), proceedings will usually be transferred to the defendant's nearest county court. This will mean that the hearing will take place there. If the defendant has moved far away, this might affect the decision on whether or not to take legal action. However, it is likely that travel expenses for attending the hearing could be recovered if the claim is successful.

If there is a genuine dispute over the amount of money owed or whether it is owed at all, it will usually be a good idea to seek mediation. There is now a very wide range of mediation services (see Resources section for details). The advantages of involving outside mediation are clear. The costs are often lower than they would be if lawyers were instructed for litigation. Furthermore, disputes are frequently resolved more quickly. Some firms of solicitors providing mediation services guarantee to have fixed an appointment within 28 days of contacting all the parties.

* * *

2.4 Are there any legal problems in accepting gifts or legacies from clients?

Therapists are often faced with a situation where a client wishes to offer a gift, perhaps at the end of therapy. However, this is an area that could give rise to a number of difficulties. The nature and purpose of the gift, as well as the circumstances in which it is given, should be carefully considered. The position will also depend on the manner in which the gift is made. If it is in the form of a legacy, it would be necessary to consider disputes that may arise over the validity of the gift in the will.

The ethical position also needs to be considered, since this may have an impact on any legal issues. Generally, any counselling or psychotherapy relationship is seen as a relationship of trust. The intimate nature of the relationship will mean that any decision taken by the client in the course of therapy may be influenced or coloured by the therapeutic work being done. Feelings of gratitude towards a therapist will often be generated by the therapy.

The possibility arises that these feelings, which might be a natural and positive part of the therapeutic work, will be exploited by the therapist. Accordingly, it is not a good idea to accept personal gifts of substantial value during the course of therapy. Some practitioners, particularly those working from a psychodynamic perspective, might be inclined to refuse any kind of gift, however small, just so that clear boundaries are maintained. However, perspectives will probably differ on this point, since the therapeutic issues raised may be, in reality, diverse and unpredictable.

The important question to ask is whether a practitioner is potentially exploiting a therapeutic relationship for personal gain (or whether the practitioner's professional body might see it this way). Most codes of ethics deal with this possibility. If a gift, beyond merely a token, is given during the course of, or after, therapy, this could later leave the client feeling exploited. In this case, it is likely that a heavy burden will fall on the practitioner to show that accepting such a gift was not an opportunistic use of the therapeutic relationship.

The nature and purpose of the gift is relevant. For example, if the gift is received as a donation to the therapist on behalf of a charitable organization, and no personal benefit arises for the therapist, the possibility of ethical sanctions may be less. The question might still arise, however, as to the therapist's involvement in such a donation. It is still possible that the client might feel later that they would not have made such a donation had it not been for their feelings of gratitude towards the therapist. All of this will depend on the particular facts of each case. As far as the legal position goes, this is likely to raise some complex issues of trust. It would not be practical to give any detailed introduction to this area of law, since a lay person could easily misunderstand the complexities involved here. In our view, the possibility could arise that a substantial gift made by a client to their therapist could be retrieved later by the client. There are probably a variety of legal arguments that might be deployed to achieve this.

First, a claim may be made in terms of the contract between the therapist and the client. This is where the ethical position might have a bearing. If it were clear that the receipt of the gift was an unethical exploitation of the therapeutic relationship, this exploitation might give rise to a claim for damages for breach of an implied term of the contract. The implied term in the contract would be the therapist's duty, derived from the accepted ethical position, not to financially exploit the client. The damages sought in this case would be the value of the gift, possibly with interest.

A second legal argument might be based on the principles of equity. This would most likely arise in cases where the client may suffer from some kind of psychiatric disorder or other mental impairment or disability. To understand this kind of claim, it is necessary to understand the difference between the legal concepts of 'law' and 'equity'. It is not practical to give a detailed explanation of this complex area of law. It would be enough to say that the cliché 'possession is nine-tenths of the law' does not take account of the principles of equity, where the true intentions of the parties are more relevant.

If the gift were in the form of a legacy in a will made out to a former therapist, the relationship of the testator (the person writing their will) to the beneficiary will most likely be relevant to any challenge to set aside the gift. If, for example, a person had changed their will and redirected a substantial amount towards their therapist, possibly at the expense of the client's close family, this might become a circumstance that would 'excite the vigilance and suspicion of the court'. Challenges to such a gift might focus on the ability of the testator to appreciate the testamentary act. These sorts of arguments would be enhanced by any history of mental illness. However, the fact that a person seeks psychotherapy would not necessarily be an indication that they were suffering from mental impairment, since many people clearly choose to seek psychotherapy primarily for reasons of personal growth.

It is wise, therefore, to avoid accepting gifts or legacies of other than token value, such as a card or a small memento, in order to avoid any potential suspicion of a breach of trust with the client or their estate. Remember, though, that from an ethical perspective unwillingness to accept a gift may be interpreted by the client as a rejection. Practitioners should therefore explain why it is inappropriate for them to accept such gifts and remind their client that the client's gratitude is recognized in the payment of fees (if relevant) and by the client's ongoing commitment to the therapeutic process.

* * *

2.5 Could a therapist be sued for *failing* to do something (for example not setting a clear contract) rather than by *actively harming* a client (for example by exploiting them in some way)?

This question hints at whether there is a distinction in the United Kingdom between malpractice (actively doing harm) and negligence (causing harm by failing to do something). Actively harming a client could be the basis for a criminal prosecution, if the therapist had, for example, intentionally physically harmed a client with overenthusiastic and unskilled massage or 'rebirthing' techniques. Whether there is a distinction to be drawn between malpractice and negligence probably derives in part from ethical principles, that is the distinction between the duty of beneficence (doing good) and the duty of non-maleficence (not causing harm). The distinction also seems to be more strongly based in United States law than in the United Kingdom. In the United States, for example, therapists have been sued for failing to end contact with the client appropriately, or for failing to minimize the risk of suicide. The crucial reference point here is the notion of the therapist's duty of care. In the United Kingdom, courts essentially ask the same question in every case of alleged wrongdoing: has the therapist fallen below the duty of care required of them? The law recognizes that a breach can occur by doing something and getting it wrong, or by failing to do something which there was a duty to do. The wider and more extensive is the duty of care, the more opportunity there is for therapists to fall foul of their responsibilities to provide a professional and effective service to clients.

In UK law, the courts have tended to take a narrow and more restrictive view of the therapist's duty of care than their counterparts in the United States. This may be because the courts here have historically taken part of their role as maintaining a strong grip on the potential uses of litigation. The danger of opening the floodgates, referred to previously, is often used by judges as a background reason for not deciding in favour of a particular case, unless there are compelling reasons to do so. This has tended to act as a brake on the widening use of the law to cover all types of dissatisfaction concerning counselling and psychotherapy.

There are two main types of law that could be used by a client as the basis for legal action, if dissatisfied with the therapy provided. The first of these is via an action for breach of contract, which would be fairly simple to use. Where there was a clear contract between counsellor and client, which met the necessary legal requirements, action could be taken for failing to comply with it. A contract requires several conditions for it to become legally binding. These are:

- **capacity**: parties must be 18 or over
- **intention**: the clear purpose of the arrangement is to create a legal contract
- **agreement**: evidence of a decision, such as signatures
- **consideration**: exchange of money or goods for services

If a therapist failed to provide the therapy paid for in advance by the client, or if the client failed to pay for the therapy already received, action to enforce the contract is fairly straightforward via action through the small claims court, a branch of the county court (see response to Question 2.3 for further discussion). Not every aspect of the therapy needs to be specified in the contract. Some conditions may be explicitly specified in the contract, as an express term of the contract. The therapist might have specifically undertaken to provide skills training for the client in self-hypnosis but then not actually provided this service. This failure could be a breach of an express term of the contract and may be actionable by the client. If the therapeutic work was believed to be of unusually poor or ineffective quality, the client could also take action given that it will be an implied term of the contract that the service should be of reasonable quality. Express and implied terms of a contract can apply whether it is a written or verbal contract, although it becomes markedly more difficult to establish what was agreed verbally after the event! Without being unduly defensive, counsellors should record all important discussions, such as the terms and goals of therapy, in writing, both as a useful aide-memoire and as proof of what has been agreed.

These kinds of 'failure to deliver' apply under contract law. Again, it is worth pointing out that any overambitious promises to 'cure' a client's target problem or to make them feel substantially better within a set number of sessions could well result in an action for breach of contract (see Question 2.2 for more discussion on this topic).

The other main area of law, which is relevant here, is the law of negligence. This is based on the concept that each person owes a duty of care to avoid causing harm to their neighbour by act or omission. Again, the law uses the word 'neighbour' in a legalistic way to denote anyone who is likely to be affected by another person's actions. It does not imply that a client can only sue if they live in geographical proximity to their practitioner. Rather, it means that a client can sue in negligence if it can reasonably be expected that a client would be adversely affected by the counsellor's actions. This principle has developed into a substantial body of case law relating to medical negligence. These principles would be applied, by extension, to a counsellor and or psychotherapist alleged to have caused harm to a client.

The grounds for bringing a negligence action are:

- the existence of a duty of care between practitioner and client
- breach of that duty
- resultant foreseeable harm to the client, arising as a direct consequence

In order to constitute negligence, the foreseeable harm must be serious in nature, not transient or trifling. In order to claim damages, the client would have to demonstrate that the breach of the therapist's duty of care resulted in, for example, a psychiatric illness, such as clinical depression or post-traumatic stress disorder, rather than simply in feelings such as anger, hurt or disappointment. The harm could also be in physical form, such as premature labour caused by unsupervised and inappropriate physical group activities caused by trust exercises involving substantial or robust physical contact.

Establishing a duty of care between a therapist and client is relatively straightforward. Whenever a practitioner offers to give, and a client agrees to accept, counselling in return (usually for a fee), a duty of care will arise. What is less clear, and much more open to debate, is of exactly what elements this duty of care might consist. This is where the area of causing harm by omission might be particularly relevant.

The proper components of the therapist's duty of care would be established in court proceedings by reference to codes of practice, where they apply, and to the views of well-qualified expert witnesses. Minimum legal requirements for therapeutic practice are not laid down for non-medical therapists, unlike, say, the position of therapists who are also qualified as doctors or nurses. This leaves some aspects of the practitioner's role open to debate. For example, would a therapist be in breach of their duty of care to the client by failing to give them regular and frequent supervision, in failing to keep detailed notes of sessions with clients or, finally, in failing to refer a client to mental health services when the latter was apparently suicidal?

These questions can be answered differently, seen from a viewpoint which might be based on a broadly ethical perspective rather than one which is more narrowly based on the law. From the perspective of codes of ethics, and the possibly formal requirements of professional associations such as the British Association for Counselling and Psychotherapy (BACP), a lack of supervision might be seen as a breach of an ethical duty to maintain professional standards. Lack of recording is more problematic, as record-keeping is not a formal ethical requirement as such but rather one which may be job-related as a formal condition of employment. Failure to refer a potentially suicidal client may be criticized both from an ethical point of view and in terms of duties imposed via an employment contract, for example by virtue of working in an NHS setting. However, it would not necessarily constitute a breach of duty of care from a more narrowly legal perspective.

Owing a duty of care to a client establishes potential liability towards that client. This might be one reason for caution in assuming that a duty of care exists between a supervisor and the client of the supervisee, for example. If the duty of care does exist in the eyes of the law, the supervisor would become liable and could be sued by the client, as is possible in some parts of the United States (see the response to Question 6.5 on this issue).

All the three aspects described above – supervision, recording and appropriate referral – may be considered to be elements of good ethical practice. Whether they are necessarily parts of the therapist's legal duty of care is more arguable. A therapist might well be considered to be competent without necessarily having supervision. And if it is required, how is the frequency or adequacy of supervision to be judged? In the absence of prescribing medication or medical treatment, keeping detailed notes of sessions might not be considered absolutely essential to maintain minimal standards of competence (although it is usually prudent to keep such records, as discussed elsewhere). Not every instance of suicidal ideation by a client might require immediate referral to the relevant mental health services. The fact that a former client has actually committed suicide is not in itself evidence of a breach of duty of care seen after the event. The client may have not fully reported all the factors causing them to feel suicidal or may have been in the habit of making frequent, but apparently unfounded, threats of self-harm or suicide in the past.

The limited evidence available so far, in the form of published court reports, suggests that judges tend to take a narrow, rather than a broad, view of the therapist's duty of care. The two key cases are *Werner v. Landau*, and *Phelps v. Hillingdon LBC*. In the first case, a psychiatrist was in breach of his duty of care as a result of socializing with his emotionally vulnerable client, in the context of working with transference issues from a psychoanalytic perspective. In the judgment of the court, the breach of professional boundaries had contributed directly to the client's suicide attempt and subsequent loss of income.

In the second, more recent case, an educational psychologist was found to be in breach of her duty of care to her client, a schoolgirl, by failing to test her for dyslexia. Other professionals considered dyslexia to be the probable cause of the client's considerable educational difficulties. This breach was considered to have caused the client substantial later problems in terms of educational underachievement.

These cases are, however, rare. The courts are unlikely to find a therapist negligent for failing to do something, unless this failure involves an absolutely vital and essential aspect of competent therapeutic practice. Once again, the strongest defence against litigation is for the therapist to work within the boundaries of safe, competent and effective practice, as determined by their professional association and employing agency.

* * *

2.6 Can I be sued if a client objects that my therapeutic approach was inappropriate for their particular problem (for example by my providing psychodynamic psychotherapy rather than behavioural counselling for panic attacks)?

This question represents an interesting variation on the issue of litigation (or being sued) that is covered in Question 2.5. It is more usual for a therapist to be sued for actively harming their client in some way, for example by sexually or financially exploiting them within the counselling relationship. This question raises issues about the enormous variety of therapeutic approaches and which of these, if any, can be seen to be more 'correct', either in general terms or for specific client problems or conditions.

It also raises the issue of appropriate initial assessment, and referral, of the client. Clearly, assessment is not a term that is equally acceptable to all schools of counselling and psychotherapy. However, the concept of assessment does include a stress on the importance of accurately perceiving the nature of client's experience at an early stage in the relationship, whether or not this includes the use of more formal means of assessment or diagnosis. A bereavement counsellor, for example, may miss the high level of hopelessness and desperation that indicates that their client is actively suicidal. Another counsellor may pick up a client's low mood but miss the periodic onset of uncontrollable elation, which would suggest a bipolar, rather than a unipolar variant of depression.

Successful case law in the United Kingdom on this particular type of alleged negligence is thin on the ground. There is case law from the United States, however, in the case of *Osheroff v. Cabot Lodge* that does fit this situation very closely. In this instance, a highly distressed client was admitted to a psychiatric unit and diagnosed as having a narcissistic personality disorder. He was offered psychodynamic psychotherapy, which seemed to have little immediate effect in relieving his obviously high anxiety level. The client was then transferred to another psychiatric hospital, re-diagnosed as having manic depression and prescribed medication, which apparently rapidly eased his condition. The client then attempted to sue the first unit for misdiagnosis and for inappropriate treatment of an established psychiatric illness. The case was settled out of court. This means that the client and the owners of the first unit reached an agreement on a level of financial compensation to be paid to him, without the judge making a formal decision on the case. This also means that the case did not set a precedent in United States law, although lawyers in the United States and United Kingdom are rather fond of quoting it as an instructive example.

What they may not always mention is that the client was himself a doctor well versed in diagnosis and psychiatric treatment and therefore ideally placed to sue on these particular grounds.

This last point perhaps underlines the limited likelihood of a repeat situation arising in the United Kingdom. Any future client would need to be similarly well-informed about appropriate forms of treatment or therapy for specific problems or to have ready access to expert advice. The enormous diversity within counselling and psychotherapy is such that even experienced practitioners may be unaware of all of the various therapeutic approaches on offer or unsure of which of these would be most appropriate in the client's particular circumstances. Again, it would perhaps be hard for the client to prove that the particular form of counselling adopted had actually proved to be harmful as opposed to failing to help them sufficiently to deal with an anxiety problem, for example. (This assumes that the therapist had not promised, unwisely, that any therapy provided would be guaranteed to overcome a specific problem, such as frequent panic attacks.) If the type of therapy provided had lasted an inordinate length of time, without any perceptible improvement in the client's condition, it might be alleged that this constituted poor professional practice and was potentially financially exploitative and therefore unethical. However, from a legal perspective, this would not necessarily amount to evidence of causing the client direct psychological harm as such.

What the question does raise is the need for therapists to possess some skills in early recognition of those kinds of deep-seated problems that require specialized help. A relationship counsellor, for example, might decide early on in the counselling work that a male client could really benefit from psychosexual counselling to help deal with a specific problem, such as premature ejaculation. The counsellor would need to be aware of the wide range of therapeutic interventions relevant to the client, the most appropriate agencies available to offer help and the research data, which could indicate which approaches might claim to be particularly suitable. However, this somewhat 'technical' approach to assessment, referral and treatment does not sit easily (or at all) with the pronounced pluralism of contemporary therapeutic culture. One counsellor's identified 'target problem' may simply be, for another, an expression of a more deep-seated underlying emotional or relationship problem, which requires longer-term therapeutic work.

The legal test for negligence sets a high threshold for establishing harm. The burden of proof is on the client, who has to show clear evidence of harm, as opposed to simple dissatisfaction with the chosen type of counselling approach. It will be much harder for clients to sue practitioners on this basis if they have been actively involved in negotiating the form that the therapy will take. This highlights the need for practitioners to be very clear about how they work and about the clients' responsibilities, so that the latter can reach an

informed decision about whether or not to embark upon a therapeutic relationship. Failure to provide this information could be considered as
unprofessional. It could also be argued that a therapist who did not give this
information would have failed to secure the client's informed voluntary consent. Therapists need to work to the best available evidence base of clinical
effectiveness, but this may not be always be straightforward or obvious at the
time. For example, it may be difficult for the therapist to distinguish clearly
between anxious, ruminative thoughts and a more pronounced obsessive-
compulsive disorder. Failure to 'assess' or select the therapeutic approach
with the strongest evidence base is unlikely to constitute evidence of negligence as such. It might provide material for a complaint to a professional
association, but such an example of practice would also still not necessarily
provide conclusive evidence of actual therapist incompetence as such.

A powerful example of this kind of client dissatisfaction is provided by
Anna Sands, in her personal account of receiving psychotherapy (*Falling
for Therapy*, Macmillan, 2000). She took part in psychodynamic psychotherapy, which she experienced as being cold, impersonal, frustrating
and, ultimately, counter-therapeutic. In fact, she had claimed to have experienced a 'nervous breakdown', or acute emotional crisis, with which the
therapy seemed unable to help her cope. She later went on to have a completely different experience with person-centred counselling, which felt
much more equal, supportive and empowering. She tried to explore her
feelings about this first unsatisfactory experience of therapy with her former therapist's professional association, but, in turn, seemed to find this
latter process as baffling and unproductive as the original therapy itself.

Could a client in this situation sue for inadequate diagnosis and assessment, for the use of an inappropriate form of therapy or even for the
failure to establish a 'good enough' therapeutic alliance? Briefly, the
answer has to be, generally speaking, that it is not possible to sue on this
basis. The client needs substantial evidence of the therapist's breach of
duty of care and the resultant foreseeable psychiatric harm directly caused
by the breach. Simple dissatisfaction with a therapist, and with their
approach, however acute, or even the onset of significant emotional distress, will not necessarily count as proof that the therapist has necessarily
been incompetent and damaging to the client.

Moreover, the elective and voluntary nature of the majority of counselling relationships, as an expression of the client's autonomy,
presupposes that an informed, competent person is exercising self-respon-
sibility by taking part. Unless the client is actually being compelled to
engage in the therapeutic relationship, for example in order to comply
with the terms of a court order, the client does have the choice of leaving
therapy when it does not meet their expectations.

* * *

2.7 Can I be sued by the parents of my (adult) client? They are claiming that I am responsible for implanting in her mind false memories of sexual abuse as a child.

This question, and its answer, are related to the earlier discussion in Question 2.6, in that it concerns the therapist's duty of care. In this particular situation, it relates to whether a duty of care exists towards someone who is, presumably, not directly involved in the therapy itself, but towards a third party. In this case, the third party comprises the *parents* of the client. Action for redress could follow two distinct paths. The parents might seek to bring an action against the therapist for breach of contract. However, this particular route is blocked under the concept of 'privity of contract'. This means that, as the parents are not parties to the contract for therapy, they cannot, therefore, bring an action on these grounds. The second route, which is more feasible, would be to try to sue the therapist for damages caused to them as a third party, as a direct result of incompetent therapy. In this case, their claim would seek to claim damage caused by the therapist through fostering ideas in the client that the latter had been sexually abused by their parents, when there was no real substantive evidence for this.

The key point of reference here is the *Ramona* case from the United States. In this situation, a young woman with an eating disorder recovered what were possible memories of being sexually abused by her father. In part, the clarity of these initially vague memories was assisted by the use of a drug, sodium amytal, which was administered by a psychiatrist working with the therapist. The father was asked to join a therapy session, where he was directly confronted with the accusation of abuse, which he strenuously denied. He then successfully sued the therapist, psychiatrist and the clinic where they both worked for damages to his reputation and for his loss of employment, which had allegedly occurred as a direct result of the accusations made.

This case has been much discussed in therapy circles in the United States, as it is set in the context of a much wider debate about the validity of recovered, as opposed to false, memories of sexual abuse. It is unlikely that such a civil case could be brought against a therapist in the United Kingdom. From a legal point of view, the issue is one of third-party liability, that is the extent to which a therapist owes a duty of care to a third party who could be directly affected by the process or outcomes of therapy with the client. The law in the United Kingdom has traditionally been reluctant to define a duty of care as existing beyond that which is owed to the immediate client. The law in the United States, and particularly in California, where the *Ramona* case was originally heard, has taken a much more liberal view of the duty of care, by extending it to progressively widening circles of potential claimants. Arguably, even in the *Ramona* case, the father's right to sue the therapists involved had a strong basis, in that he was invited to join the therapy session to hear the accusations. He therefore had a much more direct personal connection with the therapy in question than might otherwise have been the case. In being asked to join the therapy, it was held by the court that the practitioners owed a duty of care to him, separate and additional to the duty of care owed to his daughter.

To date, there does not seem to have been a similar successful legal case brought against a therapist on this basis in the United Kingdom. (This is distinct from those cases where *complaints* have been made to professional associations concerning false-memory allegations.) What has developed in its place is the use of 'false memory' as a successful defence strategy, in both civil and criminal cases. In these situations, the defendant's solicitors have managed to discredit the case brought against the alleged abuser by challenging the role of the therapist in appearing to foster unsubstantiated charges of abuse.

The other main development on these lines has again taken place primarily in the United States, labelled 'retractor action'. In these cases, a client in therapy has recovered memories of possible abuse, made accusations against her parents as being responsible for this abuse and then broken off all personal relations with them. In some situations, this might entail bringing a civil case for damages against the parents or giving evidence to the police in order to start a criminal prosecution. In some cases, a process of reconciliation develops between the client and their estranged parents, with the result that the legal case is later dropped. The client, retracting the original accusations against the parents, brings a civil case against the *therapist* for professional negligence, in fostering false memories of abuse that have caused substantial distress and disruption to the family as a whole.

The grounds for a successful 'retractor action' by a client need to follow essentially the same lines as that for any type of professional negligence. This is the standard threefold test, namely:

- the existence of a duty of care to the plaintiff
- breach of the duty of care
- resultant foreseeable harm arising as a consequence of the breach

The duty of care, in this context, would centre on the kind of therapeutic responses used by the counsellor in exploring the original memories of abuse. These memories may have prompted the client to start therapy or may have actually surfaced later during the therapeutic work. Therapists would be unlikely to use drugs, as occurred in the *Ramona* case, outside of a clinical setting, where medication is only prescribed and supervised by a medical practitioner. However, in any civil or criminal case, the defence would mount a robust challenge, via cross-examination, to the therapist's competence to work with survivors of abuse, the extent and status of their training in this field and the validity of methods used to elicit, explore or validate possible memories of past abuse. Reference to a sound evidence base, for example, in tracing the potential links between a client's current eating disorder and previous childhood sexual abuse would also be important. Familiarity with authoritative reports on false and recovered memories by professional associations, such as the British Psychological Society, British Association for Counselling and Psychotherapy, and the Royal College of Psychiatrists, would be an obvious precaution (see Resources section for details). The practitioner should be aware that certain therapeutic techniques, such as hypnotherapy, 'inner child' work and guided visualization, might be seen by a court as being overly suggestive in influencing the client. Lawyers would challenge the basis for any assumptions held by the therapist, such as the relationship of past sexual abuse to the client's current emotional difficulties.

From a legal point of view, the therapist clearly owes the client a duty of care to work in a fully professional, competent and sound manner. This is particularly important when working in the very sensitive area of exploring past abuse and its current effects on the client (see Walker, 2003, in this series). The therapist's professional accountability can ultimately be put to the test via legal action for alleged damage caused to the client. However, the difficulties facing the client in proving a case of professional negligence against their therapist remain substantial, whether as couched here in terms of 'retractor action' or on any other basis.

* * *

2.8 If I follow my common sense, keep reasonably up to date and stick to well-established professional boundaries, how likely is it that I will ever be sued by a client?

Any therapist who follows the suggestions here is unlikely to be successfully sued by a client, given the current legal climate. This is not to say that a client will not *threaten* to sue the therapist and involve the therapist in substantial worry and a significant amount of work that will be needed to respond properly to the case. The law as it stands provides very solid defences for therapists who work conscientiously, competently and within established professional guidelines for practice.

This continues to be the case, even with the advent of a more entrepreneurial approach by lawyers aimed at encouraging clients to litigate on what is known as a 'conditional fee', or, more popularly, a 'no win, no fee' basis. Here, a lawyer will agree to take on a case, which the client might otherwise not be able to afford to bring. In return, if the client is successful, in the United Kingdom the lawyer receives an increased fee, or, in the United States, a percentage of any damages won. Because the lawyer is bearing the financial risk if the case fails, the tendency is to take on only those cases that have a high probability of success.

Therapists might simply breathe a sigh of relief to know that the real risk of being successfully sued by a client is fairly slight. However, it is worth also knowing what this view is based on and how the therapist's competence would be judged if it ever came to a court case.

The client's case for bringing litigation against a practitioner has already been outlined above, namely foreseeable damage to the client directly caused by a breach of the therapist's duty of care. What is less clear is how the latter's standard of professional practice will be judged. In other words, how do the courts distinguish between a competent and an incompetent therapist? And how might this be affected by the huge (and growing) variety of different therapeutic approaches on offer?

The standard applied in judging whether a therapist falls below an acceptable level of competence is the well-known *Bolam* test, as used in medical-negligence cases. Under the *Bolam* test, based on a famous medical case heard in 1957, the question to be asked is whether the standard of practice was that of a reasonably competent practitioner. Another way of putting it is whether the practice was consistent with mainstream or well-established approaches. Evidence would need to be provided – possibly by referring to professional codes of practice, or, more likely, via the evidence of acknowledged experts in the field – that the therapist's practice was consistent with that of a reasonably competent practitioner. The therapist's defence of their work is, therefore, largely by reference to peer expectations of what would be considered to be 'good enough' practice.

Therapists should be relatively comforted by the fact that professional-negligence law has generally been more supportive of professionals than of consumers. This is because the law only requires a health professional to act 'reasonably competently'. This is a relative, or normative, defence rather than one appealing to the notion of 'best possible practice', for example. It could be that standard practice itself might not be totally beyond criticism or might even not be based on the latest research, for example. This has been the situation in some cases of medical negligence. More recent case law (the *Bolitho* case) has strengthened the requirement that the practice be not simply in line with the norms of the profession but, in addition, that it must also be rational, justifiable and accountable as well.

Whereas in the past, the courts have invariably deferred to professional opinion (on occasion demonstrating undue deference to the medical profession), the actual decision as to whether the practitioner's standard of care has been satisfactory belongs to the court. The views espoused, or actions undertaken, by a practitioner not only have to conform with the norms of the profession but the practices have also to be objectively judged to be reasonable. This marks a subtle judicial shift away from the paternalistic professional standard towards a more consumer-orientated patient standard of care.

The main example of the use of the *Bolam* test to therapeutic practice is in the case of *Werner v. Landau*. Here, the therapist was alleged to have precipitated a suicide attempt by his female client, by entering into a 'social' relationship in the middle of two phases of psychotherapy. Using the *Bolam* test, the question was whether this was consistent with the norms of the method being used, that is a psychoanalytic approach. The evidence was clear that the attempt to combine a social and a therapeutic relationship was judged to be unsound and unprofessional practice. It was seen to be completely at odds with the strict norms and boundaries of the espoused method, psychoanalytic psychotherapy. While sympathetic to the therapist's rationale, the court took a clear view that this practice failed the *Bolam* test. The therapist was therefore guilty of professional negligence towards his client. What is interesting about the judge's decision is the relatively informed and sympathetic discussion given to the issues of working with transference within the psychoanalytic approach, surely something of a milestone in English legal history!

Use of the *Bolam* test may provide a strong system of peer defence for practitioners working within the mainstream of established practice. However, one danger could be that it might be seen to penalize unfairly those approaches which are innovative or which take a different approach towards therapeutic work. A therapist using a minority approach could easily be subject to criticism by expert witnesses, simply on the grounds that they were using a new, rather than a more established, approach. This argument has already arisen within medical-negligence litigation. In the *Maynard* case, following on after *Bolam*, it was further decided by the courts that it was not sufficient to prove that one approach was negligent simply by finding expert witnesses to criticize it as being a minority approach. It would be perfectly acceptable for a therapist to use a minority approach as long as their practice was consistent with the norms of that particular school, given, of course, that this approach was not perceived to be detrimental to the client. The courts argued, sensibly in the circumstances, that not to recognize the validity of alternative competing models would be to punish innovation and reward orthodoxy, and thus put a legal brake on the development of new thinking.

The implications for therapists from this case law should be clear. Practice is legally defensible by referring to the standards that are clearly consistent with whatever approach has been adopted. Failure to abide by the specific requirements of the model may then be used to try to establish proof of harm caused to the client.

A few words are worth adding to this generally comforting outline. The *Bolam* test applies to the standard of the ordinary practitioner. If a therapist puts themselves forward as an expert in a particular field, perhaps in working with symptoms of post-traumatic stress disorder, they will be judged against the higher standard to be expected of an expert, rather than that of an ordinary, practitioner.

In contrast, and somewhat curiously, the trainee therapist is judged, however, not more leniently on the basis that they are not yet fully qualified but according to the standard of a competent practitioner. The legal analogy is with the learner driver. The law does not treat a learner driver more sympathetically than a qualified driver when it comes to dangerous driving – both are held to be responsible for their own errors. In medical case law, the inexperienced junior doctor is judged against the level of competence applying to their post, regardless of whether they have been in that position just for 24 hours or for a whole year.

The implications of the trainee standard of practice need to be thought through carefully by training organizations in the field of therapy. Student and trainee therapists carry the same level of liability for their work as qualified, competent practitioners. Where the beginning therapist is in post as a trainee psychologist, for example, the job specification should spell out that the level of practice or responsibility required will be significantly less than that of a qualified practitioner.

Finally, therapists will be relatively safe from being sued if they keep reasonably up to date with current research and best practice. The notion of 'common sense' in the question as a safeguard is more questionable, however. The logic of the *Bolam* test would suggest that practitioners need to demonstrate consistency with, and competency in, their chosen approach, rather than simply refer to intuition, gut feeling or 'common sense' as a guide to safe practice.

* * *

2.9 What level of protection should I be looking for in a professional indemnity insurance policy?

Most practitioners, considering the potential legal liabilities of their practice, tend to think in terms of negligence and the duty of care. While this kind of liability is more common amongst doctors and most other professions, the position is different with psychotherapy and counselling. In order to establish a claim of this kind, it is necessary to show that there has been damage which a court can measure. This damage is most often either financial or physical. However, the kind of damage that might result from therapy will rarely be financial or physical but rather a subjective experience of damage suffered by the client, which will be difficult to prove empirically.

Inappropriate sexual contact will probably allow the court to make an assumption that real psychological damage has occurred. There is research that could be relied on to substantiate these grounds, together with comparisons which could be made with American court decisions, which often have little difficulty in awarding damages for this kind of claim. However, other kinds of emotional suffering will be less easy to prove, short of a psychiatric diagnosis of a recognized mental illness.

In addition to proving damage, there is the requirement that such damage must be actually caused by the negligent act. Again, to prove such things in a way that a court could be satisfied in law would seldom be possible. Any pre-existing mental health problems, such as evidence of clinical anxiety or depression, might well be taken as proof that the damage claimed existed *prior* to the alleged negligent act and accordingly would not be found to have been caused by the therapist. For this reason, negligence is probably not the only important type of claim that an insurance policy would cover. There are a number of other kinds of liability that do arise, and it is important that a practitioner's insurance covers these.

First, it is often the case that therapy is conducted in the practitioner's own home, or in premises which they use for their practice. In this case, 'occupier's liability' needs to be considered. Occupier's liability is governed by the Occupier's Liability Acts of 1957 and 1984, which impose a duty of care towards people who visit the occupier's premises or land. The 1957 Act covers those who visit lawfully, and the 1984 Act covers some limited circumstances involving non-visitors or trespassers (mainly children). The duty is mainly to protect people from injury or loss arising out of the negligence of the occupier towards their safety. Practitioners should therefore take steps to ensure the safety of visiting clients from such dangers as slipping and falling, electric shock and injury from projecting nails, sharp edges or unsafe structures. Fire, gas and electrical safety advice can also usually be obtained from local authorities.

The importance of making sure that insurance covers these kinds of liabilities is as important for clients as it is for the counsellor or therapist. Unfortunately, there are very few no-fault compensation schemes. If someone suffers an injury which requires a substantial pay-out to cover such things as nursing or home care costs, it is in the client's interests that this pay-out should not be dependent on the practitioner's financial means to cover such an award. Personal-injury claims can sometimes amount to many thousands of pounds.

If other people are employed by practitioners (for example as cleaners or office staff), another area that might be relevant is 'employer's liability'. These liabilities arise in a number of ways and relate mainly to the safety of employees. In this context it would also be important to consider potential liability for such things as unfair dismissal, as well as gender or race discrimination.

Another area that has recently become more important is liability for libel and slander. Practitioners are often drawn to making verbal or written comments about their colleagues, which might attract such liabilities. This is enhanced by the perennial tendency for schisms in psychotherapy schools or movements. Psychotherapists frequently have heated disagreements with each other and accusations of defamation are, sadly, not uncommon. It used to be the case that anyone considering taking legal action for defamation needed first to be in possession not only of a good case but also of a small fortune (usually in six figures) to cover the legal costs.

All that changed with Section 8 of the Defamation Act 1996. This allows an action for defamation to be taken without the necessity of an expensive trial by jury. The procedure that was envisaged and has since been created is unlike a normal trial and is called 'summary disposal'. It is only possible to follow this approach if the claim is limited to £10,000. This new procedure has since been brought into force and is set out in Part 53 of the new Civil Procedure Rules. It can take roughly three months, which is very quick and inexpensive, when compared to the usual time it would take to prepare a defamation action for trial.

In the field of psychotherapy and counselling, the likely defendants to defamation claims are not going to be tabloid newspapers, and the level of damages would probably be much lower. Accordingly, it would seem likely that the new summary procedure would be more appropriate and affordable to potential claimants. For this reason, it becomes necessary to ensure that any insurance policy covers defamation, particularly if the practitioner intends to publish articles or books. Another thing to check is whether or not the policy covers complaints panels. It is far more likely that a practitioner will be involved in a complaint heard by their professional association than be taken to court. Some professional indemnity insurance cover specifically *excludes* the cost of legal representation at complaints panels, in order to avoid the process becoming 'top-heavy' with lawyers and barristers. Another area often excluded from cover is the cost of any legal representation involved in arguing a case in court against the disclosure of client records. This is because the therapist ordered to disclose records is in the position of being a *witness* rather than an actual party, to the case.

Some policies only cover the therapist in the case of actual litigation, where the therapist is directly involved as a party, that is as claimant or defendant.

Most insurance policies are designed to cover such matters as legal claims against the practitioner based on the duty to use reasonable skill and care and other matters relating to the contract with the client. Therapists need to ensure that they are also covered for the legal costs of defending a claim as well as for any damages which might be awarded.

It is worth bearing in mind that there will often be a 'deliberate act' or similar clause which prevents the practitioner from claiming for liabilities arising out of actions which the therapist should know are unlawful or which might expose them to legal action. This is to prevent the policy being used unfairly by the therapist as a kind of immunity from wrongdoing, such as initiating a sexual relationship with a client in the knowledge that the insurer would cover the costs if the client were to sue.

In summary, practitioners should always practice with due care and skill. Being insured will usually also carry with it various duties owed by the practitioner towards the insurer. It is imperative to contact the insurer as soon as it becomes clear that any kind of legal claim might be made. If the therapist does not do this, they might lose their cover. Therapists should also always let insurers know their full circumstances and requirements in writing at the time of taking out the policy.

CHAPTER 3

The law in specific contexts

Much of the law that is relevant to therapists depends upon the context within which they are working, such as for an Employee Assistance Programme (EAP) or primary care. This chapter explains how employment issues, including self-employment, have a bearing on the legal position of the counsellor or psychotherapist. The liability that counselling organizations have for employees, trainees/students and volunteers is also covered, including protective measures, such as insurance policies of various kinds for therapists who work as volunteers or on a self-employed basis.

3.1 As a counsellor working for an Employee Assistance Programme, I am required to give out basic legal information, which I feel ill-equipped to do, even though it comes from a manual with a disclaimer for any liability. Should I really be doing this?

There is nothing wrong with helping people learn about their legal rights and obligations. Over the years, great efforts have been made by the legal system to peel back some of the unhelpful mystique that surrounds the law and the giving of legal advice. It is now very common to find legal information available in a wide variety of settings. Indeed, the more that individuals are helped to understand the basic principles and ideas, the better. There are numerous books and leaflets available that are also intended to provide such help.

Having said this, if a person has a specific problem about which they might possibly take legal action or if they might be on the receiving end of complaint that might end up in court, this is a different matter. Basic legal ideas very rarely apply exactly to a given situation, since the realities of even the most straightforward life situations are rarely simple. To meet life's complexities, legal rules are qualified by a huge number of other legal ideas, and every situation has to be assessed carefully on its many merits. However, knowing and understanding the basic ideas of the law is better than knowing nothing.

The process of assessing the legal position in any given case starts with an assessment of the kind of factual information that might be relevant to the problem. Even the simplest of situations carries with it a vast number of facts that the person affected might feel are important but which, from a legal perspective, are not necessarily relevant. Equally, there will be a large number of facts that might seem unimportant to the lay person but which, in fact, might be crucial to the matter. Knowing the basic legal ideas certainly helps focus the search for the relevant information. The more a person knows how the law might approach a situation, the better they are able to understand what the law might require of them and others.

Accordingly, a distinction needs to be made about the kind of advice being given. General information, which carries with it an appropriate disclaimer and explains clearly its own limits, must be seen as a positive, professional service to consumers. It is important that such information be properly checked through, to ensure it is accurate and that those who are disseminating it are cautioned about speculating or expanding on its content. If someone has a specific or potential problem, they should seek proper professional advice. This is where the danger of inexperienced advisors providing ill-founded legal advice comes in.

There are a number of ways in which individuals can get advice, the most well-known of these being via the Citizens Advice Bureau (see Resources section for headquarters address). If the matter is pressing and such advice cannot be taken in time, possibly for an imminent court hearing, adjournment should be requested to allow advice to be sought. It is most often the case that court hearings are scheduled to allow a person to obtain such advice. Most procedures require specified periods of notice and formal documents giving such notice. If court orders are granted in the absence of one side of a dispute, there will always be an opportunity for both sides to attend court for a reassessment of the position in light of the other side's evidence.

Sometimes it will be necessary for someone to represent themselves in court. This may happen if they cannot afford professional representation. Much has been done in the court system to accommodate such people. The judge will usually be particularly sensitive to the position of an unrepresented person in court, that is a 'litigant in person' (see the response to Question 7.7 on this topic).

As regards employment issues, these are usually dealt with by employment tribunals. These procedures are specifically designed to make life easier for those who represent themselves. Complaints are judged by panels, consisting of a chairperson, who is a lawyer, and two other lay members. One of the lay members is from an organization usually representing the interests of those employed (for example unions) and the other is from an organization experienced in the employer's view (for example personnel departments). There is no restriction on representation and anyone can be represented by anyone else. Accordingly, it is often the case that lay advocates appear in court as well as professionals (solicitors or barristers).

The atmosphere of a tribunal is less formal than a court setting, although many of the same rules of procedure and evidence are used. The process can be initiated by filling in a form (called an 'IT1') and sending it to the tribunal. This form, together with a booklet giving detailed help on various matters, is available from any tribunal office or Citizens Advice Bureau. In addition to this, there are various leaflets, forms and other information booklets that cover specific areas of advice.

The most useful advice, which can be given to anyone who might find themselves in an employment tribunal, is to keep detailed notes of all significant transactions, including names, dates and exactly what was said. Needless to say, all relevant documents should be kept safely in one place and in good order. As far as possible, transactions should be conducted in writing and copies kept. The kinds of documents that are often useful include complaints or grievance procedures, company-policy documents, notes written at the same time as events in question, copies of timetables, logbook entries, notes of any telephone conversations and emails. It is also important to keep a record of contact details of any potential witnesses or other people who might be involved. Success in tribunals is often based on reliable and accurate record-keeping. This sort of advice can be invaluable and has no legal implications, since it is simply good sense. It is also good to bear in mind that there is usually a three-month time limit for bringing a claim in the tribunal. Again, this is advice that could only help a potential complainant.

* * *

3.2 My counselling agency will only let me work with children under 14 with their parents' permission. I feel that this actually puts many young people off, when they desperately need someone to talk to. What is the law on this issue?

Many counsellors and their agencies seem to be unclear on how to resolve this issue. They may even be somewhat nervous of alienating parents by seeming to exclude them from knowing about any counselling that their children may be receiving. The legal issue at stake here is that of the right of a young person under 16 to confidential counselling, regardless of parental knowledge or consent. (Young people aged 16-17 have a right to agree to medical treatment and a corresponding right to confidentiality, broadly on a par with adults aged 18 and above.) The law varies here in different parts of the United Kingdom. Young people in Scotland have clear rights set out in the Age of Legal Capacity Act 1991. In England and Wales, the legal position is determined by case law rather than by statute.

The key case here is that of *Gillick*. Victoria Gillick wanted an assurance from her local health authority that none of her daughters under 16 would be seen as patients, for example to ask for, or receive, contraceptive advice without her express agreement. When the health authority refused to give this undertaking, she took the case to court. In the House of Lords, three law lords endorsed the right of the health authority to give confidential medical advice to young people under the age of 16, under certain conditions.

The law lords spelled out the reasons for their decision, stating that the restrictive notion of parents' rights over children had been in marked decline for some time. Rather than having their rights being fixed absolutely by chronological age, children should be seen as acquiring the rights of adults by degrees. The young person's right to confidential medical treatment therefore depended upon their possessing a necessary level of understanding and maturity rather than upon their having passed a specific birthday.

The decision about whether a young person has this sufficient level of understanding in any given treatment context rests upon the informed professional judgment of the healthcare practitioner. Guidance on assessing the needs of the young person and the appropriate response is provided by a section of the decision known as the 'Fraser guidelines'. These require the practitioner to try to persuade the young person to involve their parents. However, if the young person refuses, medical treatment can be provided in the case of abandonment or emergency, or where the young person understands the implications of the treatment proposed, is likely to engage in behaviour with serious consequences affecting their physical or mental health, and if their welfare requires the treatment. For the purposes of counselling, *Gillick* concerns two key issues, the first of which is the right to consent to medical treatment independent of parental wishes. The second strand of the *Gillick* decision concerns the right to confidentiality, which is to be maintained whether or not treatment is provided, unless there are overriding child-protection concerns.

The Children's Legal Centre has correctly concluded from the *Gillick* judgment that the right of the young person under 16 to confidential counselling is as much at issue here as their right to confidential medical or contraceptive advice. In the absence of reported case law, counsellors working with young people under 16 can provide confidential counselling by adapting the Fraser guidelines to their own specific circumstances. Some agencies base their practice firmly on their understanding of the *Gillick* principle. Other agencies, particularly those working in schools, adopt a much more cautious approach, citing the need to work in partnership with parents as well as with children. This may stem from a confusion about obligations towards parents assumed to correspond to being *in loco parentis*, a piece of Victorian case law dating from the last century. This requires school teachers to care for their pupils as would a 'careful father', a principle adapted by degrees to 'careful parent' in subsequent case law. The concept carries a strong subliminal suggestion that, in acting for parents, schools should be mindful of parents' wishes and concerns. Offering a child-centred counselling service for pupils without specifying a need for prior parental consent could be seen to run counter to this approach. In one version of the argument, parents have rights as well – including a right to family privacy and a right to be involved in decisions about their children. Providing confidential counselling to children without parental agreement would surely count as a major infringement of the rights of the parents, to say the very least, according to this view.

This argument is persuasive but mistaken. Case law has shown that parents do not have a strong case in claiming an infringement of their parental rights by organizations such as social services. Under the Children Act 1989, the concept of parental rights has been decisively displaced by that of parental responsibility. This is a set of powers and duties that can be determined by the courts and, for example, acquired via a court order by a key figure in a child's life, such as a grandparent. The emphasis carried by this concept is much more on the duties and responsibilities involved in caring for children rather than with an untrammelled notion of power and authority over them.

In many sectors of the law, the rights and needs of children are now considered separately from the wishes and choices of their parents. This is true in the case of child protection, family proceedings and complex decisions regarding medical treatment. *Gillick* builds on these developments within the law in recognizing that young people have a right to confidentiality and to consent to medical treatment, independent of parental wishes, if they have sufficient understanding of the issues concerned.

Case law after *Gillick* has complicated the essential simplicity of this position, that children who have sufficient maturity and understanding may consent for themselves as though they were adults. This has perhaps added to the nervousness of those counsellors and agencies unsure of their ground in providing a confidential service to young people. Several high-profile cases have involved extremely acute dilemmas over the apparent right of young people to *refuse* consent to medical treatment which adults had decided was in their best and, indeed, in their *immediate*, interests. In one situation, a girl of 16, and therefore actually *over* the *Gillick* threshold, refused to accept a move to a behavioural unit specializing in treatment of her condition, anorexia. Instead, she preferred to continue in a therapeutic relationship with her psychotherapist, despite growing concerns about her weight loss and impending irreparable damage to her internal organs. In another situation, a 15-year-old girl, and therefore potentially *within* the *Gillick* framework, refused to take her anti-psychotic medication, against the advice of concerned adults. In both cases, the courts intervened to overrule the decisions of the young people concerned. The outcome was that a young person under 18 could *consent* to treatment but any refusal, even if made be a competent minor, could be decisively overturned by the consent of one person with parental responsibility.

For many, this appeared to run counter to the spirit of the *Gillick* principle. What point is there in the law allowing competent minors to agree to treatment but not to refuse it? In fact, both these and other similar cases simply illustrate the willingness of the courts to protect young people against self-harm in extreme or life-threatening situations requiring immediate decisions. In the vast majority of situations concerning the right of the young person to confidential counselling, the *Gillick* principle remains intact. The agency referred to in the question above is, therefore, on doubtful ground in refusing to counsel young people under 14 without parental consent. Any counselling offered on the *Gillick* principle clearly has to be carefully assessed as being appropriate on an individual, case-by-case basis. However, the blanket rule referred to in the question above is disadvantaging at least some young people under 16 by preventing them from receiving a properly confidential service. It is therefore discriminatory in limiting the young person's right to privacy, and is potentially open to legal challenge under Article 8 of the Human Rights Act 1998.

* * *

3.3 I work as an employee of an NHS Trust in one primary-care setting, and also do private counselling work in a second primary-care team. Am I right in assuming that I am covered by the Trust's insurance for both types of work?

As lawyers will tend to say about most things, the answer depends on the facts. Therapists often start from a healthy assumption of clinical and professional responsibility towards the client, which is no bad thing in itself. However, clinical responsibility and actual legal liability are not necessarily the same concept, even if there are close parallels to be drawn. If counsellors automatically translate a sense of professional responsibility for client welfare into assuming legal liability, they are arguably in danger of looking at this issue down the wrong end of the telescope.

In law, questions of legal liability arise from the prior concept of a duty of care, its breach and subsequent damage. There is a clear professional dimension to determining the content of this duty of care. The nature of the relationship that gives rise to the duty of care is largely decided in law by *employment factors* rather than by the specific nature of the professional service, such as counselling. The questioner is right in making a distinction between the two contexts of work, because these also relate crucially to different patterns of employment relationship.

Where the therapist is employed, the employing organization carries vicarious liability for the bulk of the latter's activities carried out in the course of that employment. This means that the employer will bear legal responsibility for the actions of its employees (provided that the employer was acting within the scope of their responsibility). As an employee, the therapist is protected by the employer's 'umbrella' of vicarious liability. In the case of legal action against the practitioner, say for non-intentional harm, the action would be brought against the counsellor and the employer concerned, in this case the NHS Trust.

This particular therapist has a portfolio pattern of employment, as is the case with many practitioners, with differing types of work and correspondingly different patterns of employment relationship. On a Monday, the therapist may be working as a counsellor employed as part of a team of counsellors in primary care and is thus covered by the employer's vicarious liability. On a Tuesday, the same therapist is seeing clients on a private basis, working from an office in what could even be the same GP surgery. In this setting, the therapist is paid directly by the clients. In this context the therapist is self-employed and carries their own personal liability in the case of legal action by an aggrieved client.

So far, so good. However, the picture can become increasingly complicated once the lines begin to shift from this rather neat division of responsibilities. If the therapist is working on a self-employed basis but is in reality working under the direction and control of the employing agency, then the concept of self-employment begins to look like a convenient fiction. By this, we mean that the employer may be using the policy of 'self-employment of therapists' to divest themselves of employer responsibilities (such as holiday and sickness pay, as well as vicarious liability in the event of a client suing). There is an argument to be made here that, where the nature of the self-employment is such that the referring organization in effect has employer responsibilities, the employer *does* bear vicarious liability for the therapist, despite the fact of the latter being formally self-employed. Whether this liability exists will depend upon the detail of the contractual relationship between the therapist and the primary care or NHS Trust, and the degree to which the therapist could be deemed to be working 'as if employed'. Should such a case come to court, the judge would look at the actual *reality* of the latter's working conditions and not simply rely on any written agreements.

Professional organizations in the field of primary-care counselling have highlighted this anomaly and have raised this as an issue affecting many of their members. This development is in tune with wider shifts and changes in employment law. One instance is where employers, such as colleges, have sought to divest themselves of responsibility for certain groups of staff, such as part-time lecturers, but have been effectively challenged by trade unions under European employment law. The emphasis, if anything, seems to be shifting *against* employers using employment technicalities to limit legal responsibilities associated with the direct employment of staff.

So, the answer to the question operates at different levels. At the simplest level, the therapist is covered by the employer's insurance where they are directly employed by the Trust. Where the therapist is working on a self-employed basis, the practitioner will need to carry personal liability for their practice and will require separate professional insurance cover for this work. As suggested, though, even this area of work, which is technically described as self-employed, could nonetheless be determined by a court to be an employment relationship that gives rise to vicarious liability by the employer. This would depend upon the nature and degree of the relationship between the Trust and the therapist concerned. As always, it is worth getting sound legal advice on the particular detail of the situation concerned, in order to be well-informed of the extent and limits of legal liability arising from employment.

* * *

3.4 My agency, an Employee Assistance Programme, requires that brief written reports be sent to the personnel department on each client – indicating the nature of the work undertaken and the outcomes of the counselling – on completion of their counselling. Do I have to comply with this practice?

It sounds from this question that there is an underlying concern here about a possible infringement of client confidentiality. Counselling in, or for, an organization can entail complex arrangements between the employing organization, the Employee Assistance Programme or counselling department, personnel or occupational health, the counsellor, client and supervisor. Managing the flow of sensitive client information becomes a matter of great importance. It is vital that all parties understand, and are in agreement with, the various types of information which need to be communicated, and the restrictions on such communication. This is necessary in order to avoid potential breaches of confidentiality and to comply with best practice. Setting out clear procedures for communicating client information, and maintaining confidentiality, is thus an essential requirement.

Confidentiality is a concept recognized and protected by the law on a number of different bases. The duty to keep information confidential arises from the 'special nature' of the counselling relationship – a fiduciary relationship which is based on trust. It would therefore be a reasonable expectation for client material to be kept private and confidential, unless there were overriding reasons for its disclosure or the client had given their consent for its disclosure. Confidentiality also enjoys the more recently established protection of statute, in the form of the specific regulations deriving from the Data Protection Act 1998, and the more general right to 'respect for privacy' under Article 8 of the Human Rights Act 1998.

The part of the law with most relevance to this situation is probably the protection of confidentiality afforded by contract law. Confidentiality is an implied term of any counselling contract, that is it is assumed to apply even if not specifically stated in the body of the contract. Given this situation, where the EAP is providing a counselling service of some complexity, the management of client information, including a requirement for reports back to the personnel department, may well be specified in the commercial contract operating between the organization and the EAP. Information exchange between counsellors, the EAP and other parts of the organization, such as personnel, occupational health and the audit office, can be found in many workplace settings. Information referred back to personnel or occupational health may include details of risk assessment, or of malpractice, where disclosure is authorized by a company 'whistleblowing' procedure. For example, in the police force, counsellors may relay back to occupational health information where a client is perceived to be a risk to themselves, to colleagues or to the public, by virtue of unresolved and continuing alcohol or drug dependency. This reporting policy needs to be with the clear understanding and consent of the client accessing the counselling service, in order to avoid any later action by the client for breach of confidence. This consent needs to be obtained from the client at the outset of counselling, so that it is made clear that any counselling provided is on the basis of restricted, rather than absolute, confidentiality.

A further aspect of this situation is where EAPs assert their right to *ownership* of all counselling records. In other words, the counsellor has to send in *all* written reports made while counselling clients who have been referred to them by the EAP. This practice may seem cumbersome and intrusive to some practitioners. The EAP is demonstrating its right to ownership of client information, derived here from the terms of its contract with the individual counsellor. In fact, 'ownership' is not a particularly accurate or useful term to use in this context. Ownership per se of client information is not a key criterion in terms of deciding how information is to be held. In the past, the former Department of Health and Social Security tried, unsuccessfully, to prevent client access to social work and medical files. It did this by arguing that it 'owned' the paper on which the records were written and could therefore decide on this basis to refuse client access. *Control* over, rather than ownership of, information and data processing is a more useful concept to employ here. Given the triangular commercial relationship between the EAP, the counsellor and the organization, the terms of any contract for reporting back to personnel, or for returning counsellor records to the EAP, can be set out in advance via contract, and thus acquire legal force.

The counsellor may have some ethical misgivings about the practice of reporting back to other parts of the organization on the content and outcome of the counselling provided. Given the legal basis for such information-sharing via contract, the best way of pursuing these concerns could be via their professional association. EAPs and agencies providing counselling services in the workplace may be organizational members of professional associations, such as the British Association for Counselling and Psychotherapy, where issues concerning maintaining client confidentiality are keenly debated, and policy options for maintaining client confidentiality in this context can be fully explored.

* * *

3.5 I work as a volunteer counsellor for a charitable organization. There is a new management committee in post, which is insisting that all counsellors, including volunteers and students on placement, have to take out their own insurance cover, which works out as being rather expensive. They are saying we are apparently not covered by the agency's own insurance for its own employed members of staff. Is this right?

This raises quite a common concern about insurance cover for volunteers and students on placement. It also reveals a widespread degree of confusion about the function and limits of insurance cover for counsellors. Counsellors and psychotherapists are increasingly, and rightly, aware of their responsibilities to clients. Proof of adequate insurance cover is widely seen as both a practical and an ethical requirement for good practice. Usually, this involves taking out individual professional indemnity insurance cover, which is tailored to the needs of counsellors and psychotherapists (see Resources section for further details). It is worth mentioning that there is an alternative, which is less widely known and less publicized than taking out indemnity insurance, which is the cover afforded by membership of a professional protection society. This operates on a different commercial basis from insurance companies and along lines more analogous to the medical defence organizations (MDOs), which are its closest counterpart.

The need to take out insurance has gradually become the hallmark of professional practice and is further linked with accreditation requirements in the minds of many practitioners. However, the point of taking out insurance or protection cover needs to be understood more clearly if this question is to be answered in a helpful way.

Insurance relates to the coverage of liability. Liability can be vicarious or personal, depending upon whether the counsellor is employed as a member of staff or is self-employed. Volunteers and students are not employed as such, so it might be assumed that they would *not* be covered by the organization's own insurance for staff members. However, there is an argument that, where volunteers and students are working 'as if employed', in other words under the direction, supervision and guidance of management and for the benefit of the organization, they effectively should be regarded by law as being in the same position as employed staff, for the purposes of determining liability.

This is not necessarily a case that organizations or even individual practitioners are keen to hear and accept. For some practitioners to query the need for counsellors and psychotherapists to automatically have their own professional indemnity insurance cover is to seemingly cast doubt on the received wisdom of professional associations. It might also be seen as undermining counsellors' legitimate claims for professional status on a par with other groups, such as medical practitioners. Organizations may be resistant to the argument that they bear vicarious liability for non-employed staff such as volunteers and students on placement. This might appear to challenge the previously fixed and known barriers to liability. Yet the argument for limiting vicarious liability solely to formally employed staff members – when there are basically similar, but unpaid, staff with equivalent training, responsibilities and supervision arrangements carrying out more or less identical tasks – is, in fact, rather difficult to sustain.

The answer to the question is that the agency is on dubious grounds in requiring volunteers and students to take out their own professional indemnity insurance cover, as it is highly likely that in the event of legal action these persons *would* be covered by the agency's own cover for employed staff. However, this discussion does raise a further question of what the purposes of such cover might be, other than affording a sense of 'being protected'. Membership of either professional indemnity insurance cover or of a professional protection society can provide a number of useful services (summarized in Question 2.9). These can include:

- free initial legal advice via a helpline
- the cost of further legal advice and, if necessary, representation in court
- the cost of any damages or court costs if awarded against the person insured

While the individual volunteer or student should not be *required* to take out their own insurance, there are still some powerful arguments in favour of doing so. However, this should be as the result of a freely made choice rather than in compliance with a somewhat questionable agency policy. In the event of legal action, the individual employee would be covered by vicarious liability. However, having separate personal insurance cover does appreciably widen the options available. The counsellor is not limited to the (perhaps partial) legal advice provided by the organization's own lawyers but has access to another source of opinion and information, in what is still a fairly fluid and developing field of law.

Perhaps more importantly, it is worth remembering that the interests of the organization and those of the individual practitioner are not always identical when it comes to responding to a legal action brought by a former or current client. Given the costs of responding to a threat of litigation, and the associated possible unfavourable publicity, it may well be tempting for the organization to seek to settle out of court. This may involve some form of payment made to the client who is alleging harm but without any admission of liability on the part of the organization. As a cost-saving tactic, this can make enormous sense to the agency. At the same time, though, it may well leave a question mark over the practitioner's professional reputation by denying them their 'day in court' and thus the opportunity to clear their name. Access to independent legal representation through professional indemnity insurance, or a professional protection society, increases the likelihood of the interests of the individual counsellor being fully represented in any compromise settlement rather than resulting in a decision arrived at over the head of the practitioner concerned.

* * *

3.6 My employer is a College of Further Education with, apparently, little regard for counselling confidentiality. Senior management is now requiring counsellors to report all child abuse within two hours to a 'named person' or face disciplinary measures. Can they do this?

This dilemma reflects some of the complexity surrounding the issue of reporting allegations of child abuse within certain educational settings. Further Education Colleges provide training and education for a wide range of age groups, which increasingly includes young people under the age of 16, through school liaison schemes and work-experience programmes. Colleges were formerly part of the local authority child-protection framework but then became independent institutions, at which stage legal responsibility for them became somewhat unclear. More recently, colleges have been brought within the ambit of the Children Act 1989. Further Education management is required to establish a clear relationship to their local Area Child Protection Committee under the 'Working Together' guidance. The role of the latter is to coordinate the process of reporting and responding to child abuse allegations, with clear guidelines for staff and volunteers working within member organizations. Normally, members of staff learning of alleged child abuse are required by their organization's reporting guidelines to pass on this information to a designated member of staff, who then contacts social services for investigation and follow-up. One managerial response has been for colleges and other agencies to impose on staff and volunteers a blanket system of reporting. This has the apparent simplicity of operating a clear and uniform policy, which discharges any obligations the organization might have under the law.

This does present a particular problem for counsellors, however. Teachers, lecturers and other staff may be required, via their contract of employment, to pass on information about possible abuse to a designated person, so that the social services can investigate, as they are required to do under s. 47 of the Children Act 1989. For therapists, however, the information may be disclosed by a client within the context of a therapeutic relationship, where the client aged 16-17 may be entitled to confidentiality under common law and statute or, if under 16, via the *Gillick* principle. A young person disclosing possible abuse may be asking the counsellor to keep this information confidential. Confidentiality, in this situation, is not an absolute duty under the law. However, it may be very important, for reasons of trust and the future development of therapeutic work, that the counsellor does not act immediately to break this confidence. In some cases, the client may refuse to give permission to pass the information on to the authorities. In others, the abuse may have occurred some time ago, and the client, or any other young person, may not appear to be at immediate risk of harm from the alleged abuser. The young person may simply need more time to come to terms with the implications of making the allegation and the likely effects on family and other relationships of social-work investigation and possible legal proceedings.

These factors make a blanket requirement for child abuse reporting within such a tight time-frame problematic and inappropriate for several reasons. If the abuse is current, the rationale for reporting within two hours makes sense from the point of view of preserving evidence, for example of bruising, or forensic evidence in the case of sexual abuse. This evidence may otherwise be lost or become of limited value for legal purposes. Similarly, prompt action may be necessary in some cases to institute emergency protection measures for the young person or other family members concerned. Social services staff would no doubt argue that the job of investigating allegations of 'significant harm' should be left to trained and experienced child-protection workers rather than be second-guessed or delayed by well-meaning, but inexperienced, counsellors or psychotherapists.

From a child-protection perspective, these arguments obviously have a certain validity. There is, nevertheless, a conflict here between the wider public interest in protecting vulnerable young people, prosecuting their alleged abusers and the core principle of therapeutic confidentiality. Managers in Further Education may be reluctant to accept that the position of counsellors in handling sensitive personal information is not identical to that of lecturers or support staff. However, counsellors have a distinct and separate role within the organization, which needs to be fully acknowledged and incorporated into any child abuse reporting guidelines. This needs to be contractually recognized at the start of the counsellor's employment.

This view is not simply indicative of a certain preciousness amongst counsellors or of a maverick reluctance to walk in step with the rest of the organization on key policy issues. Independent legal opinion obtained by the British Association for Counselling and Psychotherapy confirms the view that counsellors do indeed occupy a distinctive position on this issue and carry a specific fiduciary duty of trust towards their clients. This duty arises from well-established case law, namely that a duty of confidence arises where there is a 'special relationship' between two persons, such as a doctor-patient relationship or that between a counsellor and client. There is, as of yet, no statutory duty on staff in Further Education to report alleged abuse. It is simply a contractual or policy requirement flowing from the college's participation in the system of Area Child Protection Committees. If tested in court, it is unlikely that reporting as a contractual term could be held to override this professional duty of trust, that is unless such reporting had become a requirement actually imposed by statute. Therapists facing this dilemma need to be clear about the legal principles involved, which can provide a defence for their adopted stance. Pressure from management and from child-protection agencies to report in all circumstances can become intense. This pressure is likely to increase further in the shift towards a culture of reporting in the wake of the policy and organizational changes following on from the Laming Inquiry into the death of Victoria Climbie.

Independent legal opinion is clearly of value here but obviously does not hold the same authority as a decision by a court in legal proceedings. Counsellors do not hold sufficient power as a professional group to reverse the imposition of an automatic reporting policy by groups of employers, such as Colleges of Further Education. The result is something of a stand-off position, where college managers and counsellors have often failed to agree on policy on this issue. In fact, one rather cynical possible resolution to the problem has been the suggestion for colleges only to appoint or retain counsellors who are prepared to adopt a position of automatic reporting of child abuse. While this may appear to overcome the conflict in organizational terms, it does not address, or resolve, the clash of ethical principles to be found here, namely the conflict between a commitment to welfare and protection on the part of management and that of the fiduciary duty and commitment to client autonomy by counsellors on the other.

In brief, to answer the question, colleges may seek to impose automatic reporting of child abuse allegations upon counselling staff, together with other employees. There is no statutory basis for this requirement, given that the narrow terms of reference of the Children Act 1989 impose only a duty on the local authority's social services to investigate abuse, not a duty on *all* professionals to report abuse, as under the United States system. The imposition of this contractual term conflicts with the wider common law duty of confidentiality and trust and is unlikely to be endorsed by a court of law. However, in the absence of decisive case law, this remains a contentious, and so far unresolved, issue for counsellors working in a Further Education setting.

* * *

3.7 My client is considering giving up her well-paid job because of workplace stress. Can she sue her employers for this, and, if so, would I be called upon to support her case as her current counsellor? This prospect causes me some concern as I work in occupational health and am employed by the same organization as my client.

This raises dilemmas concerning personal and professional loyalty, as well as issues that are more narrowly defined by the law. A counsellor in private practice is probably likely to see their professional obligation as being towards their immediate client. A counsellor working for an organization has a triangular relationship, involving responsibility towards the employing or referring organization as well as to the client. Professional loyalties can come into conflict all too easily in this situation.

It may help to start by clarifying the legal process involved here. Employers have a statutory duty to protect the health and safety of staff, under the Health and Safety at Work Act 1974. Regulations updated in 1999 have upgraded this responsibility to include health surveillance. Often this now takes the form of detailed risk assessments concerning particular work activities. In addition to these statutory duties, employers also have a duty under common law not to cause harm to staff through acts of negligence. Prior to some landmark cases by employees in the mid-1990s, it was extremely difficult for staff to establish that they had suffered 'workplace stress'. In part, this was due to the imprecise nature of the concept of stress as such. It was also because of difficulties in translating the employees' suffering into one of the required legal categories necessary to establish psychological harm.

An action for workplace stress would be brought in negligence. As discussed earlier, this is part of the law of tort, or civil wrong, and refers to non-intentional harm. An employee needs to prove the usual criteria for any case of negligence: first, that the employer owes the employee a duty of care and, secondly, that a breach of this duty occurred. Thirdly, the most difficult ground to prove, is that the breach caused foreseeable harm to the employee. The onus of establishing each of these conditions is on the employee. The standard of proof required is that for civil law, namely that the facts are proven 'on the balance of probabilities'. This is in contrast to the more exacting standard required for a criminal case, which has to be proved beyond reasonable doubt.

So can any stressed employee, therefore, win a case by establishing that the nature of their work is causing them stress? Unfortunately for staff wanting to bring such a case, it is not that straightforward. First, many forms of work involve a degree of stress at times. The nature and level of potential stress should be pointed out to a prospective employee before they accept employment. Having accepted a stressful job, an employee cannot bring a legal case, unless the extent of the stress is unreasonable or of an entirely different nature to that which the employee implicitly agreed.

Secondly, employers cannot reasonably be expected to identify in every case those members of staff who will buckle under the strain. Thirdly, the law has not kept pace with developments in understanding psychological pressure, which acknowledges concepts of cumulative pressure as well as more dramatic instances of traumatic stress brought about by one-off incidents. Until recently, the law was fixed on the rather Victorian notion of a shock to the system, resulting in marked psychological distress of an extreme and disabling kind. This might, perhaps, follow being involved in a negligently caused railway accident. However, unless there is a physical injury involved, the law does not compensate for psychological distress, which falls short of a recognized psychiatric disorder. This would need to be diagnosed according to contemporary manuals, such as DSM IV or ICD 10, and could include conditions such as clinical depression, an acute anxiety state or the onset of post-traumatic stress disorder. There is a very long-established principle within the law that the normal emotions of grief or distress are not usually open to compensation. These are seen to be simply part and parcel of the human condition and of the normal 'ups and downs' of life. The rationale of this is to prevent a deluge of negligence cases wherever the actions of one party have left another feeling emotionally upset.

The barriers to employees winning claims for workplace stress are therefore quite substantial and hard to overcome. This is in spite of the impression, perhaps fostered by the media, of an emerging compensation culture for all workers and professionals. To be more accurate, successful claims need to prove the existence of foreseeable psychiatric injury, directly caused by breach of the employer's duty of care. This highly specific set of conditions will actually filter out many, otherwise seemingly worthy, claims.

The case which first established a precedent for claims of this kind was that of John *Walker*. He was a social-work manager, who experienced increasing levels of psychiatric distress in managing a demanding child abuse caseload, with limited support from his organization. He returned to continue his work after a period off sick, with promises of regular supervision, a restricted caseload and a greater degree of management support for his difficult work. This failed to materialize, and the build-up of work pressures led to his becoming unable to work through depression and anxiety. His case was backed by his union, Unison. The judge was convinced that his second 'nervous breakdown' was entirely foreseeable, given the unmet promises of support and his previous mental state arising from a comparable heavy workload. This decision has opened the door, if not the floodgates so feared by the judiciary, to a steady trickle of similar successful cases. Employers have increasingly admitted liability for causing workplace stress or have been found liable for such by a court. Successful cases have usually been brought by public-sector workers, such as social workers, teachers and nurses, relying heavily upon unions or on specialist firms of lawyers for support. To date, compensation, or out-of-court financial settlements, have tended to be somewhat modest, at least measured by United States standards. Recent cases heard by the Court of Appeal have set out in detail the key principles, which will apply in this kind of claim for some time to come. These principles essentially restate those applying in the original *Walker* case. It has also been made clear that employers providing a confidential counselling service for staff will have a strong and ready-made defence against most claims for workplace stress arising in the future.

Returning to consider the specific situation described in the question, the therapist here may experience a conflict of loyalties between the demands of their employer and the possibly competing relationship with the client. Arguably, the practitioner owes a primary fiduciary duty of trust to the client, in spite of any pressures that may be brought to bear by the employing organization. The client may seek to enlist the therapist's support for their legal action in a number of ways. These could include a request for access to therapy notes as supportive evidence for their claim, a request for a written report on the process, content or outcome of the therapy, or a request for the therapist to give evidence in court as a witness. Of course, the client could request one or more of these, or all three.

The organization may have in place a defensive policy restricting the therapist's freedom to support the client's case on a voluntary basis if the counsellor was currently also employed by the same organization. The client may then take steps to obtain access to therapy records via data protection law or by a court order for disclosure. The court may also issue an order for the therapist to attend court as a witness. These steps would override any objections raised by the employer to the therapist's involvement in the legal case. The therapist would then be obliged to assist the court by giving evidence to the best of their ability. In this case, the practitioner needs to avoid straying beyond their level of expertise. For example, the therapist may not be properly qualified to make a medical or psychiatric assessment of the client's psychological condition by diagnosing clinical depression or post-traumatic stress disorder. Overall, the organization needs to accept that the therapist has a parallel professional and legal duty towards the client. This may, in case of litigation, appear to conflict with the more narrowly perceived organizational interests of the employer in denying liability for workplace stress or in seeking to limit the amount of compensation payable to the client. Finally, the therapist needs to bear in mind the general issue that the stakes can be high in legal action for damages. The client, as plaintiff, may seek to challenge or discredit the practitioner's level of training, qualifications and professional expertise in order to establish the grounds for negligent 'treatment'. The client (or, more accurately, their legal representative) may also seek to challenge the efficacy or adequacy of the therapy provided by the employer in order to argue that the employer has failed to discharge its legal duty of care to the aggrieved client. It can be hard for the therapist to retain a sense of professional distance in this situation and to remember that, however unsettling this challenge may be, it is not necessarily a demolition of all the therapist may have achieved, both in personal and professional terms.

CHAPTER 4

Risk and responsibility

A primary concern for many therapists lies in the handling of risk and in negotiating challenges to confidentiality. This chapter addresses the legal aspects of professional boundaries to confidentiality. Therapists hold a crucial position of trust and also of professional vulnerability. As custodians of sensitive client information, they are sometimes placed in a vulnerable position. The classic situations involving risk of client harm to self, to others or to society at large are touched upon. These include client suicide and self-harm, child abuse and issues arising from clients' use of illegal drugs.

4.1 Are there any legal concerns in using your own home for doing counselling and psychotherapy in private practice?

Many counsellors and psychotherapists choose to practise from home. There are a number of reasons why this is popular. Reasons include the convenience of working from home, not having to waste time spent travelling to and from a separate workplace and the ability to fit clients in around domestic commitments. For newly qualified practitioners, working from home can certainly keep costs down, particularly if a therapist only has a few clients and does not feel that this can justify the expense of a separate consulting office or a full-time receptionist.

Working from home is not without its difficulties, and there are important considerations to be taken into account before using one's own home for counselling. Many of these concerns will be therapeutic – specifically, whether working from home will allow the therapist to develop optimally therapeutic relationships. This will clearly depend on personal circumstances. The following questions might come up:

- How does a partner or family feel about part of their home being used as a consulting room? Will clients be seen during what would otherwise be 'family time'? If there are children, will their coming and going be disruptive to counselling sessions or can they be made to appreciate the importance of being quiet when there is a client in the house?
- Can the therapist guarantee not to be disturbed or distracted at home? Is there a sign on the front door to discourage 'cold callers'? Can friends or visitors be dissuaded from arriving unannounced during business hours?
- Is the therapist comfortable with revealing so much of themselves to clients? Have additional transference implications been thought through, which might arise from unintentional self-disclosure? For example, will pictures of family and loved ones be removed from the office or consulting room?
- Is there adequate space to work from home, for example if a client arrives early before the finish of the previous session, is there both a treatment area and a separate waiting area? Is it acceptable for clients to use the toilet, particularly if this is in the family bathroom? Will other doors be locked in the unlikely event that a client takes this opportunity to snoop?
- Is it planned to install a dedicated telephone line and answering service? What steps can be taken to minimize out-of-hours calls? If the telephone number is in a counselling directory, what steps can be taken to avoid nuisance or obscene calls?
- Is there a dedicated computer for professional records, and, if not, is the data sufficiently secure? Is there sufficient room to store manual records and mechanisms for ensuring their safety as required by the Data Protection Act?
- Are there pets, and is it intended that they be excluded from the treatment area, or is it intended to allow them into the treatment room (for example to enhance the cosiness of the set up). Can alternative arrangements be made for pets if particular clients have a phobia or strong aversion to animals?
- Is the house sufficiently accessible to infirm or disabled clients, and, if not, what alternative arrangements can be made, such as the occasional renting of clinic space?

While these are seemingly practical and ethical issues, they have a legal bearing to the extent that they affect the therapist's ability to satisfy his or her *legal* duty of care. Remember that duty of care does not only relate to the delivery of counselling but to all the ancillary issues, which go towards forging a therapeutic relationship of trust and safety. From a contractual point of view, it would be an implied term of the contract, if not an explicit term, that the counsellor is able to provide appropriate premises for counselling.

There are a number of specific legal concerns relating to the use of a primarily domestic property for business purposes. As the owner of a property, generally speaking, a therapist has more freedom than if intending to operate a business out of rented premises. If it is rented accommodation, it is important to check whether the terms of the lease permit the setting-up of a counselling practice at home. Most landlord and tenancy agreements specifically exclude operating a business from the rented property. If setting up business from home is contemplated, the landlord should be informed, and, if necessary, new terms could be inserted into the lease, setting out and limiting the use of the property to the commercial activity proposed. The business of seeing clients ought not to involve disruption or activities that a reasonable landlord would object to, but it should not simply be assumed that consent will be forthcoming.

If the therapist owns their home or is thinking of moving to a new house, it is also sensible to check that the original deeds of the property do not forbid the use of a business. Homeowners have additional responsibilities towards anyone who comes onto their property. As previously discussed, the Occupier's Liability Acts of 1957 and 1984 impose a duty of care towards people who visit, or enter, the occupier's premises or land. Private practice is affected by the 1957 Act, which applies to an occupier's liabilities towards those who visit premises lawfully. The duty is mainly to protect people from injury or loss arising out of the negligence of the occupier towards their safety. Practitioners should make sure that any obvious dangers are removed and confirm that their indemnity insurance extends to any personal injury claims, which might be made by a client who is injured on the property.

A further implication of using the home as a business is that council tax is charged on the basis that the property will be used for domestic purposes only. If this is changed or extended to business use, the local authority must be informed, since the ratepayer will be liable to pay business rates on the proportion of the property used for business purposes. To counterbalance this, it may be possible to claim use of home as office when completing the income tax self-assessment form. Therapists can seek independent advice from an accountant as to what proportion of rent/mortgage and utilities can be offset against income. Further information on the use of home as office can also be obtained from the local tax office.

Another potential legal issue is if the comings and goings of clients cause considerable inconvenience and disturbance to neighbours. If it is planned to run group sessions or to encourage clients to take out their aggression by hitting cushions with baseball bats, consideration needs to be given to the thickness of the walls and how loud or peculiar the noise will be to others. Although it is unlikely that a counselling practice should prove to be overly disruptive, neighbours are entitled to the quiet enjoyment of their own property. Repeated infringements of this right could lead to the involvement of the Environmental Protection Officer (concerned with regulating noise levels) or an action, by a neighbour, for breach of covenant. It is worth pre-empting complaints by, for example, telling neighbours that some clients are seen at home and reassuring them that clients have been asked not to park directly outside their houses.

Sadly, a final concern is that the same privacy and seclusion that may be advantageous therapeutically may also create a risk to personal safety. Depending on the nature of the work, some clients may be volatile and potentially aggressive or even violent. Concern for personal safety must not be overlooked, and precautions should be considered to minimize the risks of harm (see Resources section for details of the Suzy Lamplugh Trust concerning the promotion of personal safety at work). It might also be necessary to think about the safety of personal possessions, especially if leaving clients unattended in a waiting room. A home-and-contents insurance may be invalidated against thefts if a therapist regularly accepts clients into the house. Additionally, when working from home and not from a clinic or healthcare centre where there are other people about, it is easier for a client to allege impropriety, such as assault, and harder to defend any such action. It is rarely going to be possible to employ a full-time chaperone, so it is important to think about sensible precautions. Further, advice should be sought from the local Crime Prevention Officer, Neighbourhood Watch Coordinator and appropriate professional organizations.

* * *

4.2 Can I be sued if one of my clients commits suicide? (I work with a high-risk client group, who frequently self-harm.)

Working with suicidal and self-harming clients can be an anxiety-producing experience for many therapists due to the potential for the client causing serious or fatal harm to themselves and perhaps even to others in actually making a suicide attempt. Not least, therapists may feel themselves to be at risk of blame, or even of litigation, in the wake of a successful suicide attempt by their client. Case law in the United States may fuel this concern, where therapists have faced litigation, initiated by the deceased's spouse or family, for an abrupt or inadequately handled termination of therapeutic contact or for failure to prevent client suicide.

The law in England and Wales is unlikely to impose liability on a counsellor or psychotherapist in such cases. The basic reference point is the Suicide Act 1961, under which suicide itself is no longer a crime. However, it is a crime to aid or abet suicide, for example through a suicide pact or by actively assisting the client via practical support for euthanasia. The law in this area was confirmed in the case brought by Diane Pretty, who sought to change the law on assisted suicide on the grounds of retaining choice and dignity in the face of her declining quality of life, caused by the effects of motor neurone disease. Here, the law lords refused her application, under the Human Rights Act 1998, to provide immunity from prosecution for her husband, were he to assist her death. This case is quite distinct from that of Ms B, where the court endorsed the latter's right to *refuse* essential medical treatment provided by a life-support machine. This was on the established grounds that Ms B had full capacity to make an informed choice on this issue, even if the outcome would be fatal in her case. Taking these two cases together, the law reaffirmed the absolute right of a patient to refuse life-sustaining treatment but restated the illegality of another person hastening a client's death.

Therapists are more likely to be concerned about the possibility of litigation by a former client's family following a successful suicide. This would be framed under negligence law, on the principles outlined more thoroughly elsewhere (see the response to Question 2.5). Essentially, this would require the client's family to establish, under principles of civil law, that the counsellor owed the client a duty of care, that a breach of this duty occurred and that harm, in this case the client's death, was directly and foreseeably caused by this breach.

The setting of the client's suicide is an important factor. Legal cases are more likely to be brought where the client has committed suicide in a secure setting, which would presumably have established protocols for risk assessment, close observation and suicide prevention. Thus prisons, youth custody and psychiatric hospitals are more obvious targets for litigation than counsellors working freelance or for non-specialist agencies. In fact, one branch of case law which has developed is that of the client suing such institutions for *failed* suicide attempts which have, nevertheless, caused the client to suffer lasting damage. For example, a patient who attempted suicide by throwing himself out of a window, and who became semi-paralysed and hemiplegic as a result, attempted to sue the psychiatrist and hospital for inadequate monitoring on the ward. The courts have, however, tended to take a fairly protective stance towards professionals in this context, arguing that a person determined to commit suicide is likely to succeed in at least making a serious attempt to harm or kill themselves. In any case, the fact of a suicide attempt is not in itself conclusive evidence of negligent care by the medical staff or by the institution concerned. More substantial evidence of a breach of a duty of care, as outlined by reference to a serious breach of agency practice or protocols, would probably be necessary to establish this. Even in this case, the courts do not seem unduly sympathetic to plaintiffs bringing this kind of action.

There remains a major barrier to action being brought against a counsellor by the family of the deceased client. For obvious reasons, the negligence action could not be brought by the client themselves, but it could, in principle, be brought by their estate. Grounds for negligence action by a third party, such as the deceased client's family, are not yet favoured by courts in the United Kingdom (again, unlike the more liberal stance adopted by the law in the United States).

The most likely outcome of client suicide will be an inquest to establish the cause of death. The coroner's court is something of an anomaly in English law, in that it is based on *inquisitorial*, rather than adversarial, approach. This means that the coroner has wide powers to compel attendance at court, to subpoena records and to cross-examine witnesses, all in order to establish the cause of death. Counsellors may be surprised to receive a court order for records of counselling, for example. In some cases, it may be in order to respond to this with an offer of a report describing the nature and frequency of client contact. In some cases, this may be sufficient information for the court. However, in other cases, the coroner will still require attendance at court to give evidence in person.

It is important that the therapist concerned gets adequate legal support prior to appearing in court, whether for an inquest, or for any court, in order to be prepared for the approach adopted by the proceedings. The purpose of the inquest is not to apportion blame (although it may well feel like this for the counsellor facing a client's hostile family). The purpose of the court is to determine the likely cause of death. In the case of suicide, the crucial ingredient from a legal point of view is that of *intentionality*, that is the clearly expressed intention of the deceased to take their own life.

A therapist, having had recent contact with their client who later committed suicide, is likely to be called as a witness at the inquest. As part of the proceedings, the counsellor will be required to give evidence of the nature of their professional contact with the deceased and perhaps to comment on the client's state of mind, particularly at last contact. Cross-examination by the legal representative's for the client's family may well prove very challenging, as the latter may wish to explore the counsellor's expertise in working with suicidal clients or to question an apparent failure to refer the client for urgent psychiatric treatment.

The therapist could take the stance of defending their decision-making by referring to a professional code of ethics. Often, the code will support the practitioner's autonomous decision-making, so far as it is based on appropriate supervision and is both ethically and professionally sound.

The most effective defence of the counsellor's practice regarding their client will be to show evidence of cogent and sound practice. Ultimately, however challenging or even distressing the experience of giving evidence may be for the counsellor, it is not a case of being sued for damages but of defending their professional reputation. As always, good professional and legal advice is an essential aspect of preparation for involvement in legal proceedings of this kind.

* * *

4.3 I work with couples in the context of domestic violence. If I feel that one partner is at risk of violence from another, what can or should I do to protect them?

The discussion on this issue runs parallel, in many ways, to the later response to Question 4.6, about an allegedly irresponsible client with HIV. Baldly stated, the law does not impose a 'duty of rescue' on citizens to intervene and protect other more vulnerable members of society. This was demonstrated by the legal action following the death of James Bulger, the toddler abducted and killed in Liverpool. Many citizens observed the child being led away in some distress by the two older boys, Robert Thompson and Jon Venables. In strictly legal, rather than moral, terms, those citizens were not judged by the court to be at fault for failing to intervene and protect the child. However, the law would, no doubt, have defended their *right* to do so, if carried out responsibly and in good faith.

The classic point of reference in discussions about a therapist's duty to warn a potential victim of violence, domestic or otherwise, is the well-known *Tarasoff* case. This took place in California in the early 1970s. In this situation, the therapist concerned was successfully sued, along with his employer, a university, for failing to warn a client's former girlfriend about credible threats of revenge. Unfortunately, the client carried out his threats and murdered his former girlfriend, Tatiana Tarasoff. The parents of the deceased then sued the therapist and university for breach of duty of care, namely failure to warn the victim. The result of the case was that therapists in a number of states in the United States are required by law to warn intended victims of any credible threat of harm made by a client. The case is more complex than this brief report can convey, and its consequences are often discussed in the professional press as though it had direct and equivalent implications for therapists in the United Kingdom.

In fact, the *Tarasoff* case raises important issues for therapists but does not have immediate implications for practitioners in the United Kingdom regarding a duty to warn potential victims of violence. The basic legal position in common law is that the citizen has a right, but not yet a duty, to report 'serious crime' to the authorities. This has been endorsed by specific case law, such as that of *Egdell*. Here, a psychiatrist breached patient confidentiality to warn the authorities of a serious risk of violence posed by a prisoner applying for early release from a special hospital. While breaking confidentiality is not to be undertaken lightly, it is defensible to do so 'in the public interest', where the greater good requires that crime be prevented or reported.

In the specific case of potential domestic violence, the therapist is under no legal obligation to warn the intended victim. However, there may be specific agency policies to follow, which provide an obligation flowing from a contract of employment rather than from the wider law as such. The therapist could warn the intended victim or alert the police, on a public-interest basis, in order to prevent serious crime. This stance would carry additional weight where there was an appreciable risk of significant harm to any children that may also be involved. This might apply, for example, in cases of contested contact proceedings. The threat of harm may not be limited to the client's former partner but could well involve children as well. Where social services investigate the risk to children as part of the overall threat of harm, the situation may be dealt with more urgently than might otherwise be the case, although this is not guaranteed.

Alongside the narrowly legal issues, there are, clearly, significant therapeutic aspects to consider. Warning a potential victim of a threat involves a reactive stance on the part of the professional concerned. Alternatively, providing information about available support and other resources, such as refuges, may be a way of empowering the person at risk to make their own choices, although this may be considered by some practitioners to lie beyond the traditional boundaries of the therapeutic role.

What happens if and when the therapist decides to report the risk to the authorities? Experience varies enormously as to the outcome of making a report to the authorities. At worst, the police may be decidedly reluctant to intervene, on the basis of limited resources or, if lacking firm evidence, of a breach of the peace or without firm evidence of an actual crime having been committed. In other cases, Police Domestic Violence Units will take a much more proactive stance, acting swiftly to protect the person at risk and to caution the person making the threat of harm. There are a number of steps an individual can take to protect themselves under the law, including taking out an injunction or initiating civil or criminal action under the Protection from Harassment Act 1997. However, these steps may not be practical or realistic, if faced with an immediate threat to life, when physical protection by the police or removal to a safe refuge are the only feasible measures.

One field where case law is developing on this topic is that of mental health practice. There have been numerous enquiries into apparent breakdowns of community care for discharged psychiatric patients, who have then committed acts of violence against family members or the public. At this level of practice, sophisticated risk-assessment protocols have been developed to inform decision-making, although this can never be an exact science. Issues of liability have also been tested in the courts concerning alleged failure to warn. UK law has yet to go down the path of *Tarasoff*, in placing an obligation on therapists to warn third parties under threat. However, the key principles underlying *Tarasoff* appear to be in place, should the appropriate case come to court. In one situation, a mother brought a case against her local health authority for negligently discharging a dangerous psychiatric patient who then murdered her child. Although the case was not successful, the judge's reasoning covered the contentious issue of 'duty to warn'. The two key concepts related to that of the victim being 'identifiable', rather than anonymous or simply one of a class of potential victims. The second criterion related to 'proximity', in that the intended victim should be realistically within the client's or patient's reach, as opposed, for example, to being the head of state of a foreign country.

In the past, the law has been reluctant to extend professional responsibilities to ever greater and greater degrees by incremental case law decisions. On the other hand, professional groups, such as the police and social services, who used to enjoy relative immunity from action for negligence, have now been brought within the scope of hostile litigation. Therapists may not yet be under a legal 'duty to warn' a third party under threat on *Tarasoff* lines, but the groundwork is certainly in place for this to change radically in the future.

* * *

4.4 Are there any legal issues involved in using touch with my clients?

The use of touch within counselling and psychotherapy can potentially give rise to legal issues. The main issue for therapists to consider is whether the touching is appropriate in the context of the therapeutic relationship. Even in face-to-face therapy, practitioners will vary widely in their use of physical contact. Some therapists may shake hands or even hug a client at the start or end of a session, while others avoid physical contact. Others may resort to physical contact where this seems the right thing to do. Touching a client to offer comfort may be a one of a number of appropriate responses in developing trust and in demonstrating empathy.

Whereas most therapeutic encounters involve a 'talking cure', various techniques, such as rebirthing, may incorporate physical touch as an integral part of the therapy. Provided a client has agreed to the intervention and the therapist acts with due care and skill, there is no reason why touching a client, in itself, would ordinarily give rise to adverse legal consequences.

The therapist's legal responsibilities in this area reflect the ethical notion of a client's right to self-determination, including the right not to be touched against one's wishes. Controlling access to one's body is central to the notion of respecting autonomy. This right to self-determination underpins the requirement of any healthcare practitioner to obtain specific consent from a client. Many therapists assume, incorrectly, that if a client has agreed to enter therapy and has presented for an appointment, this constitutes implied consent for the practitioner to do whatever they think is therapeutically appropriate. Few therapists think that clients need to sign a consent form before entering into therapy, as if they were undergoing a surgical procedure. This view is misguided. Making sure that a client understands the risks and benefits, as well as any alternatives to the treatment proposed, is an important aspect of good therapeutic practice. A consent form is merely evidence that the process of consent has been gone through. Verbal consent will suffice, although it may be useful to have written evidence of the client's consent in the event of a future allegation that something has been done without their permission.

In law, consent is the device that turns an otherwise unwarranted touching into a lawful touching. If physical contact is to be an integral part of the counselling, this should be fully explained to the client, along with any known risks and alternatives to this form of therapy, so that the client can make an informed choice as to whether to consent to that form of treatment. The need to obtain consent is just as relevant to counsellors and psychotherapists as it is to surgeons. The function of consent is to provide a client with sufficient information to make an informed choice about whether to enter into a therapeutic relationship. Information should include: what will happen in the therapy, how long the therapy is likely to be necessary, the therapeutic style and alternative approaches. If the therapy specifically involves touch or other physical activities, either with the therapist or as part of group activity, this should be specifically referred to in seeking a patient's consent.

Failure to obtain consent may result in an allegation of battery (trespass against the person), or, if the touching gave rise to harm, to an allegation of negligence. If a client were to allege impropriety, the legal question would be whether the client had given consent to being touched and whether the touching was appropriate, given all the circumstances, and in accordance with practice rightly accepted as proper by a respected body of professional opinion.

Actions in battery and negligence need to be considered separately. A claim in negligence, as we have already discussed, would be appropriate if the client could show that the counsellor used touch inappropriately. In other words, if the use of touch was in breach of the counsellor's duty of care in that it fell short of the standard expected of a reasonably competent practitioner and the therapist had caused foreseeable harm to the patient as a result. An example of such an action was a rebirthing case in the United States, where a child died as a result of asphyxiation. Such an outcome should not occur where a therapist was acting competently. Another hypothetical example might be the inappropriate use of touch on a client who had suffered extreme physical abuse as a child, triggering off persistent and disturbing flashbacks. Use of touch in such a case could be negligent if an inadequate history had been taken or if the counsellor failed to pick up on non-verbal cues from the client, such as an obvious reluctance to shake hands, persistent avoidance of eye contact or the adoption of a markedly defensive body posture.

But the alternative legal route, which protects a client *directly* against unwanted touching, is battery. This is a specific legal term and does not imply that the therapist has struck the client or even touched them with hostility. Rather, a claim in battery recognizes the absolute right of patients to decide what happens to their body and arises where the client has not given consent to being touched. The slightest touching of a client without their permission could be construed by the court as a battery, sometimes known in law as a 'trespass to the person'. Unlike the tort of negligence, battery is what is known as a 'tort of strict liability'. This means that a client, who sues a practitioner in battery, does not have to establish that *harm* was caused by the physical contact – the battery is in the *unwanted touching* itself.

Because of the implications of assault and battery in common parlance, successful actions of this sort are rare and the courts have been slow to find that the patient has given no consent at all. The sorts of situations in which battery actions have succeeded are those in which surgeons act in disregard of a patient's wishes, for example removing a woman's ovaries in the course of a hysterectomy. An action in battery could arise where the practitioner has given so little information about what they are about to do that the patient has effectively given no consent at all. It could apply where the practitioner has gone on to treat the patient even when the patient has expressly refused consent. Finally, it might be seen to have occurred where the practitioner has obtained consent to perform one treatment but exceeds the boundaries of consent and goes on to perform another procedure to which the patient has not consented. Because of the participatory nature of counselling and psychotherapy, it is hard to imagine many situations in which battery would arise within therapy, although the sudden and unexplained use of physical touch is a good hypothetical example. The more common legal action would be a claim that the client had not fully appreciated the risks involved in the use of touch in therapy, and, if they had been adequately informed, consent would not have been given.

The purpose of consent is to provide the sort of information that ordinary people would consider necessary to make an informed choice about whether to go ahead with something. To avoid an allegation of negligence, the amount of information that a client has to be given is, broadly speaking, the amount of information that a reasonable practitioner would give clients in order to help them make an informed choice. Although the rhetoric of counselling is client-centred, the law remains somewhat paternalistic, making the test what practitioners do, rather than what client-centred practice might optimally require. Nonetheless, to act 'reasonably', a counsellor would be expected to answer any specific questions and anxieties that a particular client may have on this issue.

In order to be able to agree to therapy, a client has to be aware of what is involved. This includes: understanding what form the therapy will take, how long the treatment is likely to last, what will be expected of the client and what the client can expect of the therapist, the therapeutic orientation involved, arrangements for supervision and any limits to confidentiality that might apply. Clients also need to be told about the risks involved in treatment and any alternatives. The purpose of this is not to put the client off therapy but to ensure that the decision to enter into a therapeutic relationship is properly understood and clients know what they are letting themselves in for. Legal complaints are much less likely to be initiated if clients have been fully informed in advance of any pitfalls that might occur in the therapeutic relationship. Obtaining consent protects the therapist as well as the client because, if they have given their consent, it will be harder for a client to complain that something happened that they had not been told about.

An important question for a therapist to ask is 'What does the client expect?' A useful way of thinking about this might be to ask: 'What information would I want to know before entering into a therapeutic relationship with this person?' Information must be given in a way that ensures that a client understands what is going to happen and is warned about how this may make them feel.

It is important to remember that a counsellor or psychotherapist is in a position of considerable power. A client may misinterpret the therapist's gestures or may have a history of being touched inappropriately in the past. When a client is laying themselves emotionally bare, it is likely to be even more important to them than usual to have their physical space respected. Another potential source of complaint or litigation is where a client feels that their boundaries have not been respected. The use of touch is only safe provided that the counsellor has a strong sense of creating and maintaining appropriate boundaries, which leave no room for wondering whether there was an inappropriate element to the touching. In all circumstances, the counsellor's intention must be to work in the patient's best interests and to respect their autonomy. Respecting the client's personal space is part of that requirement.

Clients from different cultures may find touch inappropriate, or even offensive, particularly from a practitioner of a different gender. Most codes of ethics stress the need for therapists to work in a culturally appropriate manner. Practitioners may worry that it is unrealistic to expect them to be familiar with the specific cultural nuances of touch for every client they work with. This will vary according to the context within which they work. It would be reasonable, for example, to expect that a counsellor who works mainly with asylum seekers, or with international students, to become familiar with the needs of particular groups of clients. In other circumstances, satisfying this important requirement will require therapists to draw on their professional skills to determine what level of touch and what sort of body language is most likely to be therapeutically productive.

Finally, therapists, as ordinary citizens, must obey the law like everyone else. Violence, or the threat of violence, is inimical to a therapeutic relationship. If a therapist threatens to strike, or actually hits, a client in anger or hostility, legal sanctions will apply. If anything, a criminal court is likely to respond more harshly towards a professional who has abused their position of trust and power to the client's detriment than to an ordinary citizen.

* * *

4.5 My former client refuses to accept that the therapeutic work has come to an end. She continues to write, leave messages on my work answerphone and to send me unwanted gifts. I feel very pressured and unhappy about this. Is there anything I can do to stop this?

Therapists need distinct skills to terminate therapeutic relationships effectively. Many clients feel anxious and unsure about therapy coming to an end, especially if the therapeutic relationship has been beneficial. The client's feelings of abandonment and prospective loss may find expression in hostility. One way to avoid difficulties of this sort is to treat termination as another aspect of the therapeutic relationship, which should be negotiated in collaboration with the client. This actively involves the client in the process of determining when the relationship should come to an end, thus providing them with a sense of control. Ideally, both the therapist and the client should decide whether the goals of their work together have been achieved and when further sessions are unnecessary. Therapists will recognize that clients may use various tactics and devices to delay this from happening and should respond to these attempts therapeutically. This will be easier to do if the goals of therapy have been negotiated with the client, since these can later be revisited as evidence of therapeutic progress.

Therapists and their clients may not always agree when the therapy should come to an end. In some cases, a client may wish to continue the therapeutic relationship, even after the practitioner feels that all avenues for change have been exhausted and the client is not going to get any more out of further counselling at this time. To continue providing therapy in such circumstances might be unethical (if not unlawful, strictly speaking), because it is not in the client's best interests. A therapist who continued to provide services could be accused of being financially exploitative, which would, of course, be in breach of their professional guidelines.

While it is critical to respect the client's autonomy, it is also necessary to safeguard one's own professional autonomy and not to allow the client's persistence to alter a professional assessment of whether the therapeutic relationship should be brought to a close. If, after having exhausted all common-sense means, a client still refuses to accept that the therapeutic work has come to an end, it will be necessary to think about various possibilities. Is the client's refusal to accept termination indicative of ongoing psychological needs? Is their unwillingness to accept that the relationship is over symptomatic of deeper psychiatric problems, including distorted perception? If so, the therapist may have a duty of care to refer the client to their GP, so that a full psychiatric assessment can be made.

Another scenario would be where the therapist takes a view that the client still has ongoing emotional needs but recognizes that it is no longer ethical, or therapeutically appropriate, for the professional relationship to continue. This might apply, for example, if the therapist is aware that the client has developed strong sexual feelings towards them, which cannot be appropriately resolved within the therapeutic relationship. In such a case, the practitioner would be ethically obliged to refer the client to another therapist, whether or not the client chooses to take up the referral.

Unwanted gifts are a common problem in counselling and psychotherapy. As discussed in Question 2.4, accepting gifts from clients at any stage of the therapeutic relationship is rarely appropriate. The nature of transference means that clients may adopt various strategies to be liked or loved by their counsellor. Gifts from a client, however small, should be discouraged for this reason. Therapists need to be firm but sensitive when a client attempts to give them gifts as a rebuff may itself be counter-therapeutic.

Practitioners should try to explain that accepting gifts is not appropriate and reassure clients that the professional reward is in seeing their client improve. This is in addition to the monetary exchange, which forms the basis of many therapist-client relationships where the counsellor practitioner offers therapeutic services in return for a fee.

Is there anything different about post-termination gifts? Again, the therapist needs to be wary about the client's motivation in proffering gifts, especially if they are lavish, beyond the client's means or of a particularly personal nature. Therapists should inform clients that they have a policy against accepting gifts at the outset of the therapy. Remember that courts may look very carefully at any valuable gift or legacy as evidence that the client was subject to undue influence. A disciplinary body may also construe the accepting of inappropriate gifts as evidence of unprofessional conduct.

Clients need to accept the professional nature of the relationship and not to confuse it with friendship. While there is nothing wrong or unusual about a client liking their therapist, it is the latter's responsibility to set firm boundaries. The question states that the client continues to write and leave messages on the work answerphone. Does this imply that this form of contact was also a feature of the therapeutic relationship? Were attempts made to limit contact to arranged sessions? A client's desire for contact and greater access could be an indication that the client has problems in respecting boundaries. While therapists should make themselves available in emergencies, or make other provisions for emergency treatment, the client needs to realize that they do not have open access to the therapist. However hard this may be to accept, they are not the therapist's only client and they must understand the latter has continuing responsibilities towards others.

Critically, the client's lack of boundaries is itself a therapeutic issue. It is the professional duty of a competent therapist to both create, and, if necessary, maintain, appropriate boundaries. The best time for establishing boundaries is at the outset of therapy. Initially, these should cover what the client seeks to gain from the counselling, what form the therapy will take, the period of time after which therapeutic progress will be reviewed, and, if appropriate, when new therapeutic goals may be set. It can also cover how much the client will be required to pay per session, including missed sessions, whether the therapist is in supervision, whether the supervisor will have direct access to client records and other circumstances in which confidentiality would not be maintained.

Additionally, non-verbal skills are required to create and maintain boundaries. This includes deciding how the room should be arranged, for example at what distance chairs should be placed, and whether physical contact is welcomed. Boundaries are designed to protect both the counsellor and the client, ensuring that the client's best interests remain the focus of the therapeutic relationship. This is an area that may usefully be discussed in supervision, including, if appropriate, steps to manage a particularly challenging client.

In this case, it sounds as if the therapeutic relationship has broken down irretrievably. One option might be to arrange a face-to-face meeting, giving the client an opportunity to be accompanied by a friend or advocate and possibly asking a member of the therapist's professional body to attend or by making use of mediation services (see Resources section for details).

If a client persistently harasses the therapist, it may be necessary to consider legal action, but, clearly, this should not be used other than as a last resort. Action has been taken on these grounds against a former client under the Protection from Harassment Act 1997. This happened in the case of a college counsellor subject to persistent, unwanted and intrusive attention from a colleague who had previously been to see him for counselling. It is important to be aware, though, that going to court is costly, both financially and in emotional terms. It could also result in unwanted publicity, which could have a detrimental effect on the therapist's practice.

* * *

4.6 What legal responsibility might I have if my HIV-positive client tells me he is practising unsafe sex without telling his partners?

This situation depends upon the therapist's supposed duty to warn third parties of any risk of serious harm. The closest parallel would be that of the *Tarasoff* case (see Question 4.3). Briefly, any citizen has the right (but not necessarily a *duty*) to inform the authorities where a serious crime is being planned or has been carried out. This would be on the grounds that it was in the public interest or for the good of society as a whole. The action could be justified in this way, despite any damage that may be done to the individual's right to confidentiality in passing on the information. A therapist might easily assume that the risk of the client's partners becoming infected with the HIV virus was so great that it would justify a breach of confidentiality, perhaps by informing the client's GP, for example. This might be prompted by the underlying concern on the therapist's part that failure to act might also lead to their being found liable for negligence by an aggrieved partner.

Taking the second point first, the law has so far been reluctant to accept that therapists, or other professionals, have extensive responsibilities towards third parties not directly involved in the therapeutic work itself.

The therapist's duty of care, and therefore their legal liability, is normally owed directly to the *client* rather than to the latter's partner or family. Thus it would be unlikely for the practitioner to face being sued by a partner for failure to warn.

The first point relates more to an ethical responsibility for the well-being of others affected by the client's behaviour. Again, the therapist might assume that, because warning partners of the risk of HIV was obviously in the public interest, this would be a justifiable step to take. This might not prove to be the case. The concept of the public interest is defined, in the last analysis, by the decisions of the courts rather than by the views of concerned individual citizens. There is always a degree of uncertainty as to how the courts will actually interpret and apply the concept of the public interest, given that it will often be in conflict with the individual citizen's rights to privacy and confidentiality.

This has been the case in one situation, where a newspaper threatened to reveal the names of two doctors working in a hospital who had been diagnosed with HIV. The judge rejected the public interest argument put by the editors in favour of publication. Instead, the judge asserted that the public interest in reassuring current and future patients about medical confidentiality was more significant. Revealing the names of the doctors would potentially undermine the confidence of the public that their medical details would be kept private and confidential. So a therapist could not automatically assume that passing on information to partners would be acceptable to a court of law. This would be in contrast to informing the police of a client's serious and credible threats of assault against a former partner, for example.

This stance is, however, contradicted by professional advice to doctors. The General Medical Council, for example, takes a clear position that a doctor may inform a patient's partner of the risk of developing HIV if the patient refuses to do so. Given that a statutorily regulated body has given the advice, it arguably carries greater weight than similar advice coming from a professional association of counsellors. However, this stance derives from the wider social responsibilities of the medical profession in reporting infectious disease, including HIV, tuberculosis and hepatitis.

The comparison with the situation in the United States is interesting. In the United States, there appear to be wider responsibilities on therapists to warn third parties of the risk of harm. One interpretation would include HIV under this category, and there has been extensive discussion of this issue in the professional counselling press.

The law in England and Wales has so far taken a more restricted view of therapists' liability for harm to third parties. This stance may reflect the ambivalence expressed within legal circles about putting the communication of HIV as an infectious disease in the same category as causing harm through a deliberate criminal assault. There has been discussion in legal circles, including the Law Commission, about changing the law to make it an offence to knowingly transmit the HIV virus. However, successive home secretaries have been apparently reluctant to take this step, when the factor of intentionality is clearly hard to establish. This is in contrast with a developing trend in European law, where successful prosecutions of individuals for passing on HIV have so far taken place in Finland, Sweden, Greece, Italy and Cyprus.

Within the United Kingdom, a similar prosecution took place in Scotland, where a former prisoner was jailed for five years for passing on the HIV virus to a former sexual partner. He was found guilty of acting culpably and recklessly by having unprotected sex with a partner, despite having known for six months that he was HIV positive. This has been followed in England in 2003 with the successful prosecution of a man for passing on a sexually transmitted disease, HIV, to two women who were unaware of his condition. The court's decision has been heavily criticized by Aids charities. The move to criminalise this behaviour is seen to compound the stigma already associated with the illness and hence to discourage future patients from seeking testing or advice.

Discussion of HIV often carries a strong emotional charge. Counsellors and psychotherapists need to be wary that their concern for the well-being of third parties at potential risk, or even a wish to minimize their own personal liability, may lead them to break confidentiality in good faith to warn the partner of a client. This step would probably be in advance of the law's perspective on the public interest as it stands at present.

* * *

4.7 My supervisor is adamant that all child abuse has to be reported because of the Children Act. My tutor, on the other hand, says it depends on the code of ethics. Who is right about the legal position?

While there is widespread and justifiable public concern about the incidence of child abuse in society, there is, as yet, no mandatory duty on all citizens or even on all professionals to report abuse. There is mandatory reporting of abuse by a wide range of professionals involved with children, from caretakers to educational psychologists in the United States, but this system does not apply in the United Kingdom. There was discussion of introducing mandatory reporting in England and Wales, as part of the review of child-care law leading up the introduction of the Children Act

1989. The suggestion was decisively rejected at that time. Current discussion following the Laming Inquiry into the death of Victoria Climbie has renewed debate about imposing new mandatory duty to report child abuse. This may signal a possible decisive shift towards a new culture of reporting affecting therapeutic work with children.

At present, however, instead of mandatory reporting, there is a much more narrowly defined duty on the local authority to investigate situations where a child is or appears to be at risk of 'significant harm'. This is a key phrase in the wording of the Act, covering both physical and mental harm. Suspicion, or evidence, of such harm to a young person under the age of 18 is normally the trigger for investigation by social services. Assessment of child abuse is carried out by social workers from the child-protection team, with a view to sharing evidence with other involved agencies, such as police, education and health services, via a case conference. One major outcome of such a meeting may be a decision to place the child's name on the child-protection, or 'at risk', register, according to categories such as physical, emotional or sexual abuse or neglect. The meeting may also decide whether to initiate care proceedings or to support a criminal prosecution of the alleged abuser.

The duty is therefore on the local authority to *investigate*, rather than on the counsellor as professional or citizen to report. Clearly, there is a close relationship between these two processes, and many social workers would argue forcefully that the role of therapists who suspect abuse is simply to report their concerns. These can then be investigated by skilled investigators, able to assess the level of risk to the child in question, their siblings and to other children at possible risk in the locality. They would claim, perhaps, that their job is not made easier by therapists who withhold critical information on the somewhat spurious basis of client confidentiality.

There are two aspects to providing information to social services. The first relates to making a report concerning suspected abuse, where the actual duties of the therapist are limited. However, there is also the element of social services perhaps contacting a therapist to follow up an enquiry. Again, the latter's duties are limited in this respect. Statutory authorities, such as health, education and other local authority agencies, are required to assist the social services with their inquiry by providing information. However, other persons are not specifically required to supply information unless so required by order of the Secretary of State.

The key policy document relating to the child-protection roles and responsibilities is not the Children Act 1989 itself, which is a rather impenetrable legal text. The key reference point is 'Working Together', issued by the Department of Health (and available on the web at: www.gov.uk/doh). This spells out the detail of child-protection arrangements to be adopted and put into practice by a local Area Child Protection Committee (ACPC).

Part of the function of these committees is to draw up local child-protection reporting guidelines for all staff in statutory organizations. Thus each school would have a designated person to whom other teachers or staff would report their concerns about a child apparently experiencing abuse. The designated person would then act as a referral point to social services.

ACPCs include statutory bodies, such as health, education, police and social services, together with specialist voluntary organizations in the field of child care, such as the National Society for the Prevention of Cruelty to Children (NSPCC). Other voluntary organizations working with children and young people may opt into the 'Working Together' framework on a voluntary basis and thus adopt their abuse reporting procedures. Therapists working for voluntary organizations outside of the statutory sector should confirm for themselves whether their own agency is governed by the ACPC procedures. If the therapist's agency is not part of the ACPC, or the practitioner works freelance or in private practice, they will enjoy substantially greater discretion in deciding whether or not to report suspected abuse. This may be particularly important where a young person is requesting that abuse not be reported immediately. This may be for what appear to be valid reasons, such as the abuse being historic rather than current for example. Where the therapist's agency operates under the umbrella of 'Working Together', any failure or delay in reporting will still be a disciplinary matter rather than constituting a breach of the law as such.

One of the difficult areas recognized by 'Working Together' is the potential conflict between the rights of the young person to confidentiality when making an allegation of abuse and the need to protect them from further abuse in the future. This dilemma is recognized in the document, which refers to the operation of the *Gillick* principle for young people under 16. The professionals concerned need to balance factors such as the age and vulnerability of the child or siblings concerned, their rights to confidentiality under *Gillick* (if under 16 and judged to be competent in this respect), the need to protect children and the need to punish alleged abusers.

There are various options open to a therapist with serious concerns about child abuse. While not under an absolute legal obligation to report, the latter could nevertheless report abuse to the police or social services on the basis that it was in the public interest. Reports can be made anonymously to the NSPCC if need be rather than to the police or social services. The latter two agencies will normally require identifying information from the person making the report.

How does this relate to the BACP's 'Ethical Framework for Good Practice in Counselling and Psychotherapy'? This stresses the need for accountability by practitioners and their adherence to a well-developed set of principles promoting the well-being of the client. Again, while under no absolute ethical imperative to report abuse, the therapist needs to have a clear set of principles and a coherent argument for whatever choice of action they decide to follow in this regard.

$$* * *$$

4.8 Are there any particular legal issues involved in working with clients who use illegal drugs?

Illegal drug use is a complex and emotive issue, particularly where young people are concerned and especially in settings such as schools or colleges. Therapists involved in working with drug users find themselves part of a much wider discourse about risk, blame and the destructive effects of recreational drug use. Drugs are divided up into legal (though harmful) ones, such as alcohol and nicotine, and illegal ones, including cannabis, heroin and cocaine. Even here, fixed boundaries are liable to shift, for example the decision to downgrade cannabis from a Class B to a Class C drug. As with issues such as child abuse, counsellors can find that their accountability and level of professional autonomy is open to challenge by the dominant themes of rescuing victims and punishing those who break the law.

In terms of reporting illegal drug use, the therapist is under no binding legal obligation to do so. However, in common with reporting child abuse, the practitioner may be bound by agency policy, via their contract and terms of employment, to pass on information to senior managers, who will then inform the police. This is a common response in schools or agencies where there is a strong protective or welfare orientation, particularly so where suspicions of drug dealing are concerned. A requirement to report drug use often applies in residential situations, such as bail hostels, where reported use of illegal drugs will count as a breach of bail conditions and may lead to the individual being returned to prison. Some hostels may tacitly acknowledge the reality of widespread drug use by their client population by referring to drug use actually *on the premises*. This may amount to a tacit acknowledgement that drugs are actually being used outside. Counsellors working in hostels need to be clear about agency policy on illegal drug use, reporting procedures and their own ethical stance on this issue, as a potential breach of confidentiality may well prove to have fatal consequences for the therapeutic relationship.

The therapist has a common-law duty of trust towards the client, which may conflict with reporting obligations not directly imposed by statute. This dilemma is partially acknowledged by policy documents on dealing with drug-related incidents in schools, which accept that parents need not automatically be informed of such incidents. In rare circumstances, counsellors could report client use of illegal drugs as a crime in the public interest. Alternatively, for young people, information could be passed legitimately to a Youth Offending Team, under s. 115 of the Crime and Disorder Act 1998. The main situation in which counsellors may feel it necessary to breach a client's confidentiality is where the client's behaviour is placing others at a serious risk of harm. The circumstances would have to be sufficiently serious to merit overturning the usual presumption of confidentiality. A situation where disclosure might be justified is if a therapist strongly believes that the client's use of illegal drugs is putting third parties at serious risk of harm. This might be the case if, for example, the client were a train driver who was addicted to illegally obtained opiates. In such a case, the risk of harm to others might rightly be regarded as overriding the normal duty of confidentiality. If the client cannot be persuaded to tell the employer personally, the therapist may feel obligated to disclose this fact. It should also be remembered that, if the client were involved in an accident, the therapist's records could be called in evidence at any subsequent trial or hearing. A decision not to alert the authorities may result in personal censure and disciplinary action.

Practitioners may have their own strong and decided views about the value of working with clients who are current users of illegal drugs, on a pragmatic basis. In a similar way, some therapists doubt the value of therapeutic work with clients currently on medication prescribed for conditions such as depression and anxiety. However, this is a professional and ethical issue rather than a stance directly dictated by the law as such.

There are two situations regarding client use of illegal drugs that do need special mention. Where a counsellor discovers evidence that a client is involved in drug-money laundering, the counsellor is required by s. 52 of the Drug Trafficking Act 1994 to pass this information on to the authorities or face prosecution. Informing the client that a report has been made could also lead to prosecution, so the therapist is obliged by statute, first, to report and, secondly, *not* to inform the client that this has been done. In reality, this law appears to be directly aimed at professionals in the world of finance, such as bankers and accountants, rather than at counsellors and psychotherapists, but it is impossible to predict with accuracy how the law may be actually applied in future. Therapists facing this kind of dilemma should urgently seek legal advice.

In residential settings, the conflict between the duty of confidentiality and the wider public interest in prosecuting users and sellers of illegal drugs has been forcefully illustrated by the *Wintercomfort* case. Here, two senior workers at a hostel for homeless people in Cambridge were successfully prosecuted and imprisoned in 1999, under s. 8 of the Misuse of Drugs Act 1971, for 'suffering', that is permitting, the use of drugs on the premises of the hostel. In fact, drug use amongst homeless people is widely recognized as a serious problem, and the hostel regularly barred known dealers from the premises, recording their names in a book. The police demanded access to this book, but access was denied by the management committee. The committee maintained that such a breach of client confidentiality would lead to homeless people becoming reluctant to use the hostel or to trust the staff with confidences. The police then obtained 300 hours of evidence of drug dealing on the premises via covert video recording and prosecuted the two staff members along with a number of alleged dealers. The two staff received heavy prison sentences, and their case became a cause célèbre amongst concerned professionals and members of the public. After a lengthy public campaign, the two were released on appeal, but the convictions were not overturned.

The case has sent a powerful, if rather mixed, message about the relative priority given by one court to client confidentiality compared with the public interest in prosecuting illegal drug users. Counsellors need to be fully aware that professional and common-law principles of client confidentiality may not be sympathetically received in court where issues of illegal drug use are concerned. The issue has continued to present real problems to therapists and service providers working in this field. Legal opinion obtained by the voluntary organization Homeless Link has pointed out some of the likely adverse consequences of proposed changes in regulations regarding drug use in residential settings, and these draft regulations have now been withdrawn.

Many specialist counselling services work exclusively with drug users. As such, they will have developed particular expertise and knowledge about working with this client group. Counsellors should make themselves aware of the various drug counselling services, so that they can refer clients on, if this is appropriate.

CHAPTER 5

Record-keeping

A major area of practitioner anxiety and uncertainty about the law relates to record-keeping and access to client information by other agencies. This chapter provides the essential information required for dealing with queries about confidentiality and data protection, including record-keeping and access to records. Access to client information can take on a more formal appearance via requests for the therapist to act as a professional or expert witness in court. Counsellors and psychotherapists are also increasingly asked to take on the unfamiliar role of writing reports for the court. The information needed to prepare therapists for dealing with these activities at an initial level is presented here.

5.1 As a client, how can I get hold of my own counselling records? And what can I do if I am not happy with what they say about me?

In the past, therapists, along with other professional groups, were able to operate a long-standing policy of denial of client access to records. This approach was buttressed by the refusal of powerful bureaucracies, such as the then Department of Health and Social Security, to allow access on the grounds of 'confidentiality' – the confidentiality, that is, of the professionals doing the recording. This approach was challenged, and ultimately overturned, by the actions of one client, Graham Gaskin, formerly in care of Liverpool's social services department. His legal case for access to his own social-work file, to discover the rationale for his frequent moves within the care system, was ultimately partly successful at the European Court of Human Rights. In anticipation of this major cultural shift, a raft of legislation was passed, opening up previously inaccessible professional recording in the fields of medicine, education and social work. The principle of access, with limited provisions for refusal of access in order to prevent 'serious harm' and to protect the rights of third-party material, has thus been in operation since the early 1990s. Within the developing jargon surrounding data protection, these latter records are referred to as 'accessible records'. They occupy a distinct position, overlaid by wider principles of record-keeping introduced by more recent law.

The key reference point concerning client access is the Data Protection Act 1998, which replaced the 1984 Act of the same name and substantially widened its remit. The impetus for the 1998 Act derives from a European Community directive intended to harmonize the flow of information and record-keeping within Europe. The legislation is based on the rights of the individual citizen to give consent to data processing, to have access to most forms of records kept on them and for systems to be transparent and accountable in law. The remit for data processing is based on, in the words of the Information Commissioner, a 'compendious definition', and deliberately so. The purpose of the Act is to regulate the widest possible forms of recording. 'Loopholes' for professionals to get round are few and far between. Data processing covers practically any form of recording, including computerized, manual, audio and video, which relates to 'an identifiable living individual'. Coding systems, which link an individual's details with their identity, are specifically covered by the Act. Disguising a client's identity, with codes or abbreviations, does not, therefore, remove that record from the powers of the Act.

One problem that practitioners may encounter with the Act is that of conceptualization. Within therapeutic culture, records are largely defined by their *purpose and content*. In other words, different types of recording are used for official agency purposes, supervision, personal reflection, training or research and publication. In general, these distinctions, in terms of the intended purpose of the records, are not useful ones in terms of understanding or applying data-protection law. Under data-protection law, records are defined, first, by their *context*, that is such as applying within social services, health, education organizations, and, secondly, by their *structure*, that is as being computerized or in the form of a manually based filing system. Within these somewhat blunt categories, data processing can take various forms, that is computerized records, manual records kept in structured filing systems, manual records kept in random order, or electronic data in the form of audio- and video-tapes.

In terms of access as a client, the first question therefore relates to the *context* of the record. If the therapist concerned was working in the NHS, the latter's records will ultimately be part of the client's health record. Client access is therefore possible, unless disclosure of the records would cause 'serious harm', either physical or psychological, to the client or to another party. Access to third-party material can be denied, but this is no longer a blanket defence against disclosure. The organization has to demonstrate provision for releasing third-party material where it is no longer possible to obtain consent by the original author, for example as a result of the passage of time. Access to health, social-work and education records should be straightforward, with well-functioning principles of access and disclosure in place. Larger organizations will usually have data-protection officers in post, who will be a useful point of reference or advice.

For clients whose therapist was not working for health, education or social services, access is governed by the wider principles of data-protection law. The client may have been seeing a therapist working for a college, a voluntary organization, an Employee Assistance Programme or by one working in private practice. The client has a right of access to records kept in computerized form, which will include the more formal records kept by the agency. The client has a further right of access to manual or handwritten records, probably the main form favoured by practitioners. Manual records that are kept as part of a 'relevant filing system' are those where client details are kept in a structured format, such as a card index, or roneodex, affording easy access to personal information. These are open to client access. However, where a therapist's sole recording consists of manual records that are *not* kept in a structured filing system but are kept in random order, these are not subject to the rights of client access. Therapists may be tempted to opt for such a recording system in order to retain the privacy of their records. This stance might well achieve that objective but would clearly conflict with the Act's evident ethos of transparency and accountability. It may well also conflict with wider ethical principles of promoting client autonomy and maintaining the therapist's fiduciary duty of trust towards the client.

In order to gain access to records of therapy, the client, first of all, clearly needs to know that such records actually exist. The processing of personal data, relating to an identifiable living person, requires client consent. The processing of certain forms of data, termed 'sensitive personal data', such as a person's mental or physical health or sex life, requires a higher threshold of 'explicit consent'. Consent, in this context, means any freely given indication of the client's wishes and implies an active process of gaining the client's informed agreement to the recording. The client can apply in most circumstances to the agency or freelance counsellor to read their own file. In the terms of the Act, the client is exercising their right to gain access to any data processing which relates to them as a data subject. The response will indicate the nature of records kept. However, where the records are unstructured manual records, the client is entitled only to minimal outline information, that is to their 'registerable particulars', with no corresponding right of access.

Organizations working within the spirit of the Act are now restricting the use of parallel or 'second sets' of client records, as these are not a part of official systems of recording and have therefore not been open to agency scrutiny or client access in the past. This may present problems for counsellors used to keeping 'a second set of notes' for use in supervision or for personal reflection. One policy may be to keep such notes only for a specified short life, that is to be destroyed immediately after use as an aide-memoire for supervision. The practice of keeping second sets of notes conflicts with the Act's principles of transparent, accountable systems of record-keeping and denies the possibility of client rights afforded by the law. Agencies may well opt to discourage the practice of parallel or covert recording, in order to minimize their own liability to challenge by clients or by the Information Commissioner, who is responsible to Parliament for the implementation of the Act.

The client has a right to know what records are kept and to access records kept in computerized form or in structured filing systems. It follows that the client has no automatic right of access to records of them kept by their counsellor's *supervisor*, even assuming that the latter's identity is known to them. Supervision records do not normally refer to clients as identifiable individuals, that is in ways in which personal therapeutic material can be linked to the client's name or other personal details.

Client access to personal records should be granted within a 40-day period, with a minimal charge for photocopying. The client has a right to a copy of the record and for the information to be provided in an understandable format. Acronyms, abbreviations and codes need to be explained to the client as necessary. Access to information relating to third parties may be denied, but, as said, this is not a blanket prohibition on disclosure of such material. The client has a right to have inaccurate data corrected where appropriate. Where damage has been caused, there is a right to compensation, but this does not extend to a right for compensation for simple distress on its own. A client may be aggrieved or upset at the use of specific counselling terminology, such as reference to a borderline personality for example. However, compensation for distress is linked to the question of *damage* caused rather than to simple emotional upset. Finally, where access proves problematic under the Data Protection Act 1998, a client could seek access under the related provisions of the Freedom of Information Act 2000, where the agency concerned is a 'public authority', such as a local authority or NHS Trust for example.

* * *

5.2 How long should I keep my therapy records for?

This is one of the most frequently asked questions faced by trainers on legal aspects of counselling and psychotherapy, reflecting the multiplicity of situations where practitioners work and the correspondingly wide variety of their roles. It also often relates, in a disguised form, to the issue of who actually *owns* counselling notes. Ownership of notes, as discussed in the response to Question 3.4, is not the crucial question for determining the length of time notes need to be retained. It is assumed here that, for the most part, the therapeutic records referred to are owned, that is are 'within the ownership, possession or control' of the agency taking responsibility for the practitioner's work.

The starting point is that there is no statutory requirement as such for therapists to keep any notes at all. This is in sharp contrast with the position of other professions, such as doctors and nurses, where careful record-keeping is a legal requirement, for example for prescribing drugs. This is in order to promote continuity of patient care and to enhance professional accountability. Therapists do not necessarily prescribe client care in the same way as these two professional groups. Furthermore, the 'treatment', as such, is relationally based rather than one that is interchangeable with other members of a multi-disciplinary team. The intensely private and personal nature of most client disclosures within counselling and psychotherapy also require circumspection in recording as well as keeping records securely.

Record-keeping is often presented as an intrinsic element of therapeutic practice, one that is assumed almost to be an article of faith rather than one open to critical review and discussion. The impact of recent data-protection law has caused many practitioners to question their own established practice in this area, given provisions of client access and the apparently increasing use of court orders to gain disclosure of records in litigation.

There are many purposes given for keeping records of counselling and psychotherapy. Furthermore, the dense literary quality of therapeutic culture often encourages the keeping of very detailed and personally revealing records. Records clearly have value within this culture for training purposes, as an aide-memoire, for use in supervision and for personal reflection. However, from a more narrowly legal perspective, what is the purpose of keeping notes?

Notes may be useful from a legal point of view as evidence of the therapist complying with their professional duty of care to the client. In other words, the practitioner's notes may provide evidence of working to accepted standards of practice, compatible with the *Bolam* principle (see Question 2.8). On this basis, the therapist's practice is consistent with the opinion of a body of competent respected professional opinion. (A counter argument here could be that the therapist could equally well discharge their duty of care *without* such notes, given that the client is not a patient under medication or treatment, and the issue of continuity of care is therefore less critical in an individual, relationally based form of therapy.)

Notes could be kept as the basis for providing a report to court, as a summary of contact or outcome of therapeutic work or as evidence of directly observed behaviour (for example panic attacks) or as an 'expert witness' report. Careful notes of interviews would provide the raw material for a subsequent report to the court, which may need to be further supported by the therapist presenting evidence in person. The court may later require disclosure of the notes used in writing the report.

Records may be required under a contractual obligation of employment. A therapist working for the NHS, for example, or working under contract to social services as a specialist in working with sexual abuse, will usually find that records of sessions and reports are the property of the agency. The latter expectation increasingly applies in the context of contracted work for Employee Assistance Programmes (see the response to Question 3.4). Failure to keep adequate notes in a statutory setting would usually place the therapist in breach of their contract of employment. Under the NHS, for instance, records are required and must be kept for prescribed periods of time. This can extend from eight years, in the case of medical records, to 25 years, in the case of patients with mental health treatment.

From a professional perspective, records could be kept for defensive purposes, in case of a later complaint by a client to the employing agency or to a professional association. Complaints procedures can vary from informal investigation, to mediation and quasi-legal formal hearings. Records kept may be useful in providing a sound defence against a complaint by a client, colleague or agency.

Data-protection law requires that records be accurate, up to date and be kept no longer than necessary. This leaves the agency, or freelance practitioner, with a greater degree of discretion as to the appropriate length of time to keep records, where no specific requirement applies under law or regulations. It also raises the question of the provisions for the protection and eventual destruction of records under secure conditions. This point has been taken up by some practitioners, particularly those in private practice, to underline the need for a professional will. In this situation, an executor, who is sensitive to the requirements of therapeutic work, undertakes to destroy client records in the event of the therapist's death, in order to avoid their misuse or any breach of client confidentiality.

One of the suggested deadlines for keeping records is prompted by the legal process itself and the relevant time limits for bringing a legal action. Therapists working on this principle might want to keep records for a minimum of six years, for defending a client action for breach of contract for example. The law sets various, and somewhat complex, time limits for starting a legal action. However, these can be extended at the discretion of the court. In one case, the delayed onset of a client's post-traumatic stress disorder resulted in a court order being made for disclosure of therapeutic records, well beyond the normal six-year time limit. The advice given by one major insurance company in the field is now to keep counselling records 'almost indefinitely' in order to cater for this (admittedly remote) possibility.

In the face of escalating court orders for records, and the more recent prospect of client access under data protection, some practitioners are now opting to keep minimal, skeletal records or even to keep no records at all. This becomes a distinct possibility, where there is no overall legal requirement for record-keeping, as discussed above, and where there is no specific agency requirement under contract of employment. The therapist who practices without records thus avoids some of the more pressing dilemmas faced by colleagues concerning potential disclosure to clients and the courts. However, the practitioner may encounter a challenge for their apparent failure to discharge their duty of care. As suggested above, it is quite possible for a therapist to work competently and ethically without records. Failure to keep records would not therefore provide immediate proof of breach of duty of care, although other practitioners may well be critical of such an approach. The disadvantage faced by the practitioner who works without records would be in providing a ready-made defence, against either legal action or a professional complaint brought by a client.

An absence of formal records might make the therapist less attractive to the courts as a source of information relevant to a case being heard. In the last analysis, the therapist could be called as a witness to give evidence, even without recourse to records. Many therapists might feel at a significant disadvantage in not being able to refer to detailed records of contact with a particular client. However, if all the therapist can do is refer to memory, the courts have to accept this. If the therapist honestly cannot remember particular events, this is all that can be recounted to the court, and their stay in the witness box is likely to be, at best, a brief one.

* * *

5.3 Besides my agency records, I also keep my own personal records for supervision and ongoing personal development. Is there a way of protecting these from disclosure or future use by the courts?

This question will be looked at from the point of view of access to client records by the courts rather than from the perspective of client access under data-protection law, which is discussed under Question 5.1. The practice of keeping two sets of notes is well-embedded in the practice of counselling and psychotherapy, in recognition of the uniquely personal nature of the therapeutic relationship and the corresponding need for practitioners to explore their own personal responses to client material in order to best serve the client. The practice has thus developed of therapists keeping one set of official or agency records, describing information available for purposes such as monitoring outcomes and for audit. The second set of notes will often include discussion of much more personal material, such as hunches and intuitions about the client, acknowledgement of the practitioner's own personal issues arising from the work and specific concerns to take to supervision. In the past, these second sets of notes have either been unacknowledged by agencies or viewed as constituting therapists' own private property and therefore remaining outside the reach of agency remit. This conception of privately owned 'second sets of notes' is challenged by recent developments in data-protection law and, moreover, by the growing interest of the legal system in therapeutic records, official or otherwise. The concept of records open to disclosure is a broad one, including audio- and video-tapes, personal reflective notes, aide-memoires and, potentially, supervision notes.

From a legal perspective, it is important for therapists to grasp some basic distinctions about the privacy of information. Most, if not all, practitioners will be aware of their legal duty of confidence to the client, arising from the special, confiding nature of the relationship of trust, if not from the specific terms of a contract as such. However, while therapists learn a great deal about confidentiality on training courses, they learn relatively little about the related concepts of 'privilege' and 'the public interest', which are actually decisive in determining questions of disclosure in legal proceedings. Privilege is the legal right to refuse to disclose material to the courts or to be made to testify about one's client. This is a right enjoyed by some therapists and social workers in the United States. In the United Kingdom, the only professionals possessing privilege are solicitors. Priests do not possess privilege and could be made to give evidence in court. Solicitors (or, more accurately, their *clients*) possess privilege, because, so the argument goes, without a guarantee of privacy, clients would otherwise be deterred from seeking legal advice. The courts, in child abuse cases, can override even this privilege, but this is a rare exception to an otherwise powerful defence against enforced disclosure.

However strongly therapists might be committed to the principle of client confidentiality, this does not amount to privilege in the eyes of the law. As one judge opined, 'confidentiality is not a separate head of privilege'. This means that professionals cannot simply claim privilege for themselves because it suits their interests or those of their clients. Wider social bodies, such as the courts and parliament, determine privilege.

The concept of 'the public interest' also needs to be understood by practitioners. The public interest, or what is good for society as a whole, takes precedence over the duty of professional confidentiality existing, say, between a patient and doctor. The public interest lies in the legal system having access to the widest possible degree of information relevant to deciding a case being heard by the courts. Concepts of individual privacy must come second to this overriding requirement. So whereas confidentiality is necessary for respecting personal and professional secrets, the courts can require that this secrecy be broken if that information is needed by the courts to decide a question of liability in civil proceedings or of guilt and innocence in a criminal case.

Therapists could maintain a number of different arguments about the need to keep personal records secret. One argument is that personal, reflective recording enables the practitioner to monitor their own practice and thus to maintain high professional standards of practice. However, personal records might be kept without the client's consent or knowledge. This practice is therefore questionable from an ethical viewpoint or from the perspective of the employing agency with overall responsibility for record-keeping.

In the past, professionals have argued strongly that permitting disclosure of records relating to clients would have an adverse effect on the quality of recording. If professionals recorded on the assumption that access was possible to other parties, such as the courts, recordings would become much more circumspect and would lose essential detail, and their overall value would decline as a result. The courts have decisively rejected this so-called 'candour' argument as a barrier to disclosure. The question of what, and how, to record is an issue for the professionals and agencies concerned, in matching accuracy and utility of recording with ultimate accountability via the courts if challenged.

Linked to this is the argument that disclosure of records will be damaging to the interests of clients or to those of the therapists themselves. Again, this is not an argument likely to impress the courts much. A client may be distressed, and a therapist much discomfited, at the release of therapeutic records into the legal process, but this consideration is not, ultimately, of primary interest to the courts.

The key criterion in deciding issues of disclosure of records to the courts is that of *relevance*. The legal phrase used refers to disclosure of records, in civil cases, according to 'the necessity of the case'. In the past, disclosure has been used to throw a wide net over potentially useful or interesting material, leading to claims that solicitors were using disclosure to mount 'fishing expeditions' for material potentially damaging to their opponent's case. The more recent approach is to limit disclosure to what is of direct relevance to the case in hand. There is an opening here for therapists to present an argument to the court of the limited relevance of their records to the proposed legal case. The records in question, for example, might deal solely with marital relationship issues, when the legal case at hand concerns a claim for post-traumatic stress disorder. This argument needs to be carefully and respectfully put, preferably by a barrister, in ways consistent with the established protocols of the court. Any failure to abide by the court's order for disclosure will ultimately constitute contempt of court, punishable by a fine or imprisonment.

One stance adopted by therapists when faced by a legal interest in their records for use in legal proceedings is to offer to write a report for the court. In a sense, this gives the practitioner a degree of control over the material to be released to the court. The report's content could be negotiated carefully with the client to minimize potential damage or distress. There are advantages to this approach but also some pitfalls. Counsellors and psychotherapists are not necessarily well-prepared for report writing by their training. Writing court reports is a specific and highly skilled activity, which is not to be undertaken lightly. The therapist needs to outline their professional standing in terms of qualification and experience, to distinguish fact from opinion and to clearly state the evidence for any conclusions drawn. The report could lead to the author being required to attend in person to present the report and to undergo cross-examination. Alternatively, the format and content of the report could lead to a court order for the disclosure of the original records on which the report was based. This would rather defeat the therapist's purpose if the original intention had been to protect sensitive client material by limiting its disclosure.

One way of limiting disclosure of process notes not required by the agency would be to adopt a practice of routinely destroying such material immediately after its intended use for supervision. This practice would be consistent with data-protection law, which requires the destruction of personal data rather than its retention on an open-ended basis. Of course, seeking to destroy process notes after a court order to produce them would constitute contempt and is not advisable, given the penalties referred to above.

Issues about the keeping and possible enforced disclosure of process records are a major source of anxiety for many therapists at present. It is vital for agencies to issue clear policy statements about record-keeping practice, in order to avoid confusion or unethical practice in this field. Agencies could, for example, adopt a policy that process notes were discouraged or, alternatively, deemed to be part of the client's overall file and thus potentially disclosable under data-protection law or via court order. Counsellors and psychotherapists in private practice would also need to adopt a policy concerning the keeping of records while enjoying more discretion in choosing the course of action to adopt. Any policy, whether by an agency or private practitioner, needs to make provision for the security of records kept, and their ultimate destruction under secure conditions, in order to comply with data-protection principles.

* * *

5.4 I have been called to court as a witness concerning my client in a case of sexual abuse alleged against her father. I don't want the defence solicitor to have access to these very detailed therapeutic notes. Is the safest thing just to keep them with me at all times in the court room?

The question suggests a notion that the more firmly that our notes are clutched to our bosom, the less chance there is of their being prised away by rapacious solicitors for untold purposes. We need to start by looking at the law's perspective on counselling notes, which is in terms of their value as *evidence*. Therapeutic notes may confirm a statement made by a client, their apparent state of mind or the date of a specific session or telephone call, for example. In this case, the defence solicitor may seek to use the therapy notes to undermine the client's credibility as a witness or to point out contradictions between dates of alleged incidents of abuse with other statements made. The records may be used to imply that the therapist has been instrumental in encouraging the client to bring an ill-founded case, that the client has been 'coached' in their evidence, or simply that the therapist is poorly qualified or inexperienced. Notes, in a sense, become ammunition in the legal context between two parties. They may be used or interpreted in ways that were never intended by their author or their subject, the client. Notes will clearly be of interest to both parties in the case, whether civil or criminal in nature, assuming that they are aware of their existence, as solicitors increasingly seem to be nowadays.

On a more positive note, records can be used in court by the therapist as witness to refresh their memory, to confirm basic details of contact and to demonstrate a thorough, conscientious and professional attitude to their work. The counsellor, as witness, can refer to notes in the process of giving evidence, once having obtained the permission of the judge. This brings the existence of the notes very firmly to the attention of all interested parties. It is likely that the status of the notes will need to be established – for example are the notes a contemporaneous record of events or were they completed at some time after the sessions described? Contemporaneous notes will necessarily carry greater weight as evidence in the eyes of the law. The notes need to be accurate about incidents or statements directly related to the case being heard. In one situation, a significant discrepancy in a counsellor's recording concerning the date of an alleged sexual assault led to the case bring dropped by the Crown Prosecution Service, leading to great distress on the client's part.

There are several pitfalls to using notes as an aide-memoire in the witness box. One is simply that, without careful preparation beforehand, finding specific sections may take time, increase the therapist's anxiety level and give an unfavourable impression to the court. Another is that, by bringing original notes into the witness box, the notes can potentially become the property of the court, accessible to the judge or opposing solicitor. Therapists may wish to avoid ending up handing over the sensitive personal material they had actually been trying to protect from disclosure. Alternatively, simply being in court with large files of client recordings will very effectively advertise their presence to alert solicitors, and this may, in turn, prompt a court order for disclosure as a result.

In short, there is very little protection against disclosure of sensitive client recordings in court proceedings, remembering, of course, that recordings can include personal notes, audio- and video-tapes, as well as official or agency records. Holding client records tightly to oneself in the court room is not likely to prove a very effective defence against their disclosure, either. Therapists who are seriously concerned about the damaging effects on their client of court-ordered disclosure should refer to the discussion on this topic in Question 5.3.

* * *

5.5 My client has asked me to write a report in support of his claim for criminal injuries compensation. If I were to agree to this, can it go wrong for him, or for me, in a legal sense?

The first question for this counsellor to ask is whether they are competent to write this report. Primarily, this will mean restricting comments to areas within the therapist's professional expertise rather than using speculation or conjecture. As in all areas of professional practice, therapists will be held accountable for their actions, so it is vital that they bear this in mind if they agree to write this report. Provided that they stick to their professional observations, there is no reason why this should put them in a difficult position. Obviously, their own professional responsibilities require them to stay with the truth and not to exaggerate the level of a client's suffering in the hope of securing them higher damages. This should be made quite clear to the client, before undertaking to write a report, in case they are harbouring the expectation that the therapist will write a report which maximizes the likelihood of a substantial settlement or damages.

In terms of accessing the client's records to write a report of this nature, the fact that the client has elicited this report means that the therapist will not be breaching their confidentiality by drawing on their case records. Both therapist and client should be prepared to be cross-examined about the contents of any report the therapist writes. It is possible that the tribunal or court might require a therapist to produce their records concerning the client, which could put them in a difficult position.

However, a legal problem might arise if the client vigorously disagrees with a report and does not want to submit it, claiming, at that point, that an unauthorized disclosure would constitute a breach of confidentiality. This might be the case if, for example, the therapist found that the client's injuries had *not* materially contributed to their current mental health problems. Such an issue arose in the *Egdell* case. In that situation, a psychiatrist was asked to prepare a report on behalf of a patient to submit to a Mental Health Review Tribunal, with a view to securing the latter's release from a special hospital. In the event, the psychiatric report concluded that the patient was still a danger to the public and that he should not be released. Because this report was so damaging to his chances of release, the patient sought to suppress the report, claiming that it would be a breach of patient confidentiality for the doctor to send the report off without his permission. The court found that the public interest in disclosure of this information outweighed the patient's right to confidentiality.

Since the professional role is to enhance a client's well-being, it is important that the therapeutic relationship is not compromised by involvement in this process. The client needs to realize that the Criminal Injuries Compensation Board may decline to make a payment or may make an offer which the client feels is derisory, given their suffering and sense of injustice. Clients should be aware of the limitations of the legal system and should also be warned of the psychological costs involved in seeking justice. A therapist should be careful to avoid causing further psychological harm to clients who may feel that they have been let down by not persuading the board of their entitlement. This could be detrimental to the therapeutic relationship.

A therapist will also need to make to clear whether there is a charge for writing this report. Writing a report on the client's behalf would certainly be extra-contractual, and therapists would be well-advised to refer to their relevant professional body to determine the appropriate amount to charge for such a report.

* * *

5.6 Can a therapist act as an expert witness in court? Do I put myself at risk in any way if I take on this role?

Therapists are becoming more involved in the legal system, and the opportunities for them to take on the role of experts are also on the increase. The notion of acting as an expert may be appealing, and even seductive, for some practitioners, as confirmation of their experience and abilities, but it is worth sounding a note of caution before opting to take on this demanding role.

There are differing types of witness within the legal system, and it is worth distinguishing what is required in the various roles. Any therapist could potentially act as a 'witness of fact'. This simply involves giving directly observed evidence that a client had attended a certain number of sessions. A therapist could also act as a 'professional witness' (more commonly known as an 'expert witness'), with the evidence including both fact and opinion, where the latter is firmly based on their professional qualifications and experience. The therapist might state that, in their opinion, cognitive-behavioural therapy was an appropriate form of treatment for anxiety arising from pressures within the workplace. Of course, lawyers acting for the opposing side will try to cast doubt on the nature of the qualifications held by the therapist, their actual value as a support for the opinion offered and the limited nature of the practitioner's professional experience. Cross-examination can be an uncomfortable experience, as very often the therapist may well feel personally undermined and attacked by the opposing counsel, when this is just part and parcel of the adversarial legal system at work.

An expert witness is able to offer an *opinion*, based on their breadth of expertise in a specific area. This should arise from their being an acknowledged expert in the field rather than simply an enthusiastic amateur, either hoping to advance a favoured cause or attracted by the prospect of fame and glamour associated with the role of 'expert'. The purpose of the expert witness is to provide 'independent assistance to the court by way of objective unbiased opinion in relation to matters within his expertise', according to the guidelines set out in the landmark case of the *Ikarian Reefer*, which involved a contested shipping insurance claim. The emphasis is on helping the court to make a decision, rather than on helping one side to win their case by selectively marshalling facts that will support one side as opposed to another.

The courts have, in the past, been somewhat wary of making use of expert evidence from a therapeutic perspective, as this has been seen to be no more complicated than the application of robust common sense.

However, the courts welcome opinion by psychiatrists, as this may be seen as coming within a medical field of expertise of diagnosis and assessment. The increasing use of post-traumatic stress disorder as a recognized diagnosis would be an example of this development. Opinions by psychologists have also been accepted in contentious matters, such as the suggestibility of claimants in 'false memory' cases. Other practitioners have been able to challenge long-established notions of common sense relating to 'normal' patterns of behaviour under severe stress, by informing the courts about the phenomenon of 'learned helplessness' as a feature of 'battered-woman syndrome'.

Clearly, the research and evidence basis of any claims made will be crucial to the way in which such opinions are perceived by the court. Anyone acting as an expert witness needs to be thoroughly familiar with the current and past research literature relating, for example, to critical incident debriefing and to the methodological strengths and weaknesses of their evidence base. Expert witnesses must also possess sufficient professional self-confidence to stand up to rigorous, and possibly hostile, cross-examination.

There is training available for therapists who are considering taking on this role. The British Psychological Society has produced a training video available for hire, and there are a number of law firms that run short courses on this topic. A format for an expert witness report is available from the Academy of Experts (see Resources section). Any therapist interested in taking on this particular role would be well-advised to have training beforehand in order to be fully prepared for what can be an exciting, if demanding, extension to their professional portfolio of skills and experience.

* * *

5.7 The local police are putting me under pressure to hand over my case notes on a client, where they are gathering evidence for a criminal prosecution for child abuse. Do I have to give in to their requests?

To answer briefly: no, not without a warrant. The police have a difficult role in upholding the law and bringing alleged offenders to justice. In their view, it may seem that the niceties of counsellor-client confidentiality must take second place to the need to protect the public, particularly vulnerable members of society such as children, and to punish and deter offenders. However, the police constitute only one component part of the justice system. In fact, unusually, the law recognizes a high degree of confidentiality of counselling records and affords them special protection from police seizure. Under s. 12 of the Police and Criminal Evidence Act 1984, counselling records are specifically *exempted* from police powers of seizure, unless authorized by a warrant made out by a circuit judge, rather than, say, by a magistrate.

The police can be persuasive, if not apparently heavy-handed on occasion, in their wish to obtain critical evidence, which may appear to play an essential role in obtaining a conviction. It is important that counsellors are aware of the specific legal protection for their records in this respect and require the police to obtain the warrant before releasing their records. It is also advised that the counsellor records all items removed by the police, for example tape recordings and floppy discs, and obtains a receipt covering all items taken away.

This may be a somewhat unlikely occurrence for most counsellors, where the police are obtaining evidence in order to bring a case to court via the Crown Prosecution Service. The probably more likely variant is a court order for disclosure, which is discussed in Question 5.3. There is some limited case law on police seizure of records, which may be of relevance. In one case, the police attempted to gain access to psychiatric records of patients in an in-patient unit in connection with a murder enquiry. The consultant concerned refused to comply and successfully contested the application in the crown court. While these were medical, rather than strictly therapeutic, records, this does set an interesting example of how the courts may be persuaded that the police's demand for access in the interests of justice will not automatically be granted by the courts.

However, in another case in Scotland, the police seized not counselling records but highly confidential HIV medical research data, which was used to convict a man in prison of knowingly passing on the HIV virus to his former partner. This prosecution was taken under a branch of Scottish law, which does not directly apply in England and Wales. However, this significant breach of prisoner/patient confidentiality was only noted as a serious matter by the medical press and received little media attention elsewhere. It therefore remains somewhat unclear how the courts will respond to future conflicts between, on the one hand, police demands for access to counselling records in the interests of justice and, on the other, the principle of client confidentiality defended by counsellors under both common law and statute.

* * *

5.8 Can a therapist decline to give evidence in court against their client, if this is really a matter of conscience? How would I claim this right if I were ever to face this situation?

Counsellors and psychotherapists take their duty of confidentiality towards clients very seriously. Any requirement by the courts, or other authority, to reveal client secrets goes very much against the grain. The professional and ethical requirement for keeping client confidentiality is matched by a legal duty of confidence under common law. This duty is not, however, absolute. Therapists in the United Kingdom do not enjoy 'privilege', namely protection from a legal obligation to give evidence in court. As one legal saying puts it, 'confidentiality is not a separate head of privilege'. In everyday language, counsellors cannot refuse to give evidence in court simply on the grounds that it would violate client confidentiality. The wider public interest in the disclosure of even very sensitive client information is judged to be more important to society than the maintenance of client secrets, unless the courts are convinced that there are strong and compelling reasons for doing so.

So, the therapist who is unwilling to comply with a court order to disclose client records or, as in this case, to appear as a witness, is in danger of being found in contempt of court, unless they comply. Contempt of court would apply to a therapist who shredded their records after an order for disclosure from the court, or to one who failed to disclose all relevant records, including for example, audio- and video-tapes, supposedly 'personal' sets of notes and records of supervision. Finally, a therapist called as a witness who refused to give evidence in person would run the risk of being found in contempt of court and could be fined or sent to prison as a result.

What may lie behind the question is a reference to the Hayman case, which has rather passed into therapeutic folklore on this issue. This concerned a situation where a psychoanalyst, Dr Anne Hayman, declined to acknowledge that the defendant was even her client, let alone to disclose confidential client material, even should the client's permission be obtained. She argued forcefully with the judge that either step would be unethical and counter-therapeutic to the transferential relationship, on which her work was based. As she claimed in a later article published anonymously in *The Lancet*, 'Justice, as well as our ethic, is best served by silence'. Whether the judge was bemused or convinced by her arguments is unclear. In any event, the result was that she was permitted to step down from the witness box without being forced to give evidence against her will.

This may be the case implied by the question, as a defence against giving evidence where it is 'a matter of conscience'. Unfortunately, the law is not generally so understanding of the needs of therapeutic confidentiality when it conflicts with the interests of the legal system. Counsellors are required to give evidence, and disclosure of confidential client records is now commonplace. Counsellors in the United Kingdom do not possess 'evidential privilege', even *after* the Hayman case. Each and every case is decided on its own merits. The judge's decision here was a demonstration of *judicial discretion* rather than one providing a firm precedent in case law, which other therapists can claim when faced with this dilemma.

There are a number of strategies that therapists can adopt when faced with a court order to reveal client records or to give evidence in court. The powers of the courts to order disclosure are very broad, both with reference to 'unused material' in criminal prosecutions, and in civil cases. In civil cases, disclosure is required according to the 'necessity of the case', according to the authoritative civil procedure rules. It is possible for the therapist or employing organization to make out a case to the judge that the confidential counselling records would not be relevant to the case in hand. A judge can peruse the records in chambers and decide whether the disclosure be limited to certain pertinent parts of the recording, disclosed in full or considered exempt from disclosure.

While this is a viable tactic for therapists to employ, which has been effectively used in the past, there is some skill and expertise in making a successful application. Advice on procedure may be obtained from legal helplines, professional indemnity insurers and professional associations. One point to bear in mind is that the cost of any actual legal representation involved, such as by a barrister to present the case to the judge for limiting disclosure, is not generally covered by most indemnity insurance schemes. The therapist is not usually a party to the case involved but occupies the role of witness, which does not normally involve legal representation. Therapists facing this situation need therefore to consider the likely costs of obtaining any such legal representation and how these are to be met *before* opting to use this approach to the courts to limit disclosure.

CHAPTER 6

Training, supervision and the law

Some legal queries are specific to core counselling and psychotherapy activities, such as research and publication or training and supervision. This chapter clarifies legal concepts, such as breach of confidence and the nature of damages for such breaches. Many supervisors are unclear about the likely limits of their liability, in terms of clinical responsibility, and their legal responsibilities for trainees and supervisees. These issues are addressed directly through relevant questions on these topics.

6.1 The fact that I am gay seems to be a barrier to my being accepted onto a particular, very traditional, psychoanalytic training scheme. Is there anything I can do about this?

Whereas anti-discrimination legislation has improved in other arenas, in the United Kingdom, discrimination on the basis of sexual orientation has, until recently, continued to be an unresolved problem. There have been strenuous moves to eradicate discrimination in its many forms. However, until the acceptance of EU legislation, the United Kingdom had no domestic provision to cover discrimination on the basis of sexuality or sexual orientation, which was comparable to the Sex Discrimination Act 1975, the Race Relations Act 1976 and the Race Relations (Amendment) Act 2000, or the Disability Discrimination Act 1995.

Employers and trainers have been able to exercise discriminatory policies largely unchecked. A candidate who is refused access to a course, or a potential employee who is not offered a job because of direct or indirect discrimination, has not, until now, had any legal remedy. Without the need to give reasons, training institutions have been able to accept or reject candidates on arbitrary, discriminatory grounds. One of the problems with covert discrimination is that it would always be possible to give an alternative justification as to why a place had not been awarded. While this may mask the real reasons, it would be hard to prove that the reason had been overt homophobia.

It goes without saying that discrimination in any form is anathema to counselling relationships and should be equally anathema to any training institution providing counselling education. To deny access to a training course to a student who is openly gay would infringe the basic values of counselling, which include a commitment to appreciating the variety of human experience and culture and respecting human rights and dignity. Current advice excludes specific mention of discrimination against prospective students, although the BACP guidelines stresses that counsellors should not discriminate against colleagues on the basis of their lifestyle, gender, age, disability, race, sexual orientation, beliefs or culture. However, to the extent that any training school is a member of the BACP, it will be expected to work within the latter's 'Ethical Framework' and apply equal opportunity policies accordingly.

Finally, however, specific legislation has been introduced in the United Kingdom to combat discrimination on the basis of sexual orientation. This has come about due to the EC Employment and Race Directives, which aim to provide a common framework of protection against unfair discrimination across Europe. EC Directive 2000/43/EC requires EC members to introduce legislation to outlaw unfair discrimination on the basis of race, sexual orientation, religion or belief, disability or age in the fields of education and training. The Employment Directive, which will introduce anti-sexual-orientation discrimination, was implemented in December 2003. The terms of the directive apply specifically to vocational guidance and training and so would apply to recruitment procedures for training schools as well as to employment. The Employment Directive applies to both the public and the private sector, with no exemptions for small organizations. The directive also applies to 'occupations', which are taken to include both employment and self-employment, and would thus cover counsellors working in either the public or private sector. It is intended that any new legislation will shift the usual burden of proof. If someone alleges that they have been the victim of discrimination based on sexual orientation, the burden of proof will be on the respondent (in this case, the training institution) to establish that their actions were non-discriminatory.

As with current legislation, differences in treatment are allowed only where there is a 'genuine and determining occupational requirement' to engage the services from persons falling within a particular group. There is also specific provision in the directive designed to enable churches and other 'religious or belief organizations' to preserve their particular ethos. While there is no definition of 'belief organization', the consultation exercises to date stress that this does not include political beliefs and is directed principally at faith systems.

It remains to be seen whether any psychoanalytic school will challenge the applicability of the directive on this ground, using the argument that their tenets constitute a belief. Whereas a person's sexual orientation generally has no bearing whatsoever on their ability to do a job, a psychoanalytic school which believed that being gay is an unresolved psychological issue might challenge the suitability of an openly gay student (especially when most courses now require students to work with clients from an early stage). Until the legislation has been in force for a while, and some of these issues are tested, it is impossible to judge how the courts would deal with such an argument. However, the directive specifically prohibits organizations claiming the religious exemption from demonstrating other forms of discrimination, including that based on sexual orientation.

On a practical level, this particular candidate may consider whether this institution is able to provide a satisfactory and unbiased education. Prospective candidates should also bear in mind that the training school is likely to impose a requirement that students undergo psychoanalytic psychotherapy, the orientation of which may also be anathema to gay students.

This is not to say that students in this position are powerless to act. If students really are convinced that their sexuality has been a barrier to admittance, they could make a formal complaint to the professional body to which the training school is affiliated. While professional bodies may have limited powers to censure or disaffiliate a training institution, rather than an individual practitioner, they might be able to exert some pressure to ensure that all approved training schools comply with equal-opportunities requirements. For the individual student, however, their efforts are probably better targeted at political lobbying, while seeking training at a more supportive institution.

* * *

6.2 Where do I stand in the law if, as a workshop presenter, one of the workshop participants claims to have been psychologically damaged by the experience (for example by taking part in a regression exercise as a form of experiential therapy)?

For the main part, we have discussed negligence in the context of an individual client suing an individual practitioner. Increasingly, however, many therapists engage in a variety of professional activities, including leading workshops. Is the duty of care owed to workshop participants the same as the duty of care owed to individual clients? As discussed previously, in negligence, a duty of care is owed towards anyone who might foreseeably be affected by a therapist's actions or omissions. This would include workshop participants and would not depend on whether or not they had paid a fee to attend. This is unlike an action for breach of contract, which would probably only be open to a participant who had paid money in return for attendance.

The issue of negligence arises whether or not the people attending the workshop are themselves practising therapists. However, a court would probably be more ready to infer that a therapist who participated in an exercise and suffered harm as a result would have been more able to decline to participate than a client receiving individual therapy. A therapist taking part in a workshop would presumably have had the resources to avoid or minimize harm, for example by stopping the exercise when they became significantly distressed. Failure to do so might be considered as contributory negligence on the part of the workshop participant.

Again, remember that, in order for a person to claim negligence, the participant must prove that the harm suffered was both foreseeable and of a serious and lasting nature. An example of harm arising might include a workshop leader failing to intervene in a group session in which a participant was subjected to sustained sexual or racial harassment, which, additionally, could infringe discrimination legislation. Similarly, if a workshop leader were to disclose personal information about a participant gleaned in a group discussion at a workshop, this could also lead to an action for breach of confidence.

Would a therapist be liable for harm if they had not organized the workshop themselves, but had been invited to lead the workshop by a private company? Since the workshop participants have a contractual relationship with the course organizers rather than the speaker, they may choose to sue the company which ran the conference rather than the individual presenter. If this happened, though, the company would almost certainly join the therapist as a potential defendant.

Informed participants should be made aware of the theoretical, but small, possibility of harm as a result of their participation, so that they can choose whether there are parts of a workshop that they would rather sit out. While it would be unusual to elicit explicit consent for conference participation (this can usually be implied by a participant's presence), a presenter should expressly ask a participant for consent to take part, for example in a guided imagery demonstration.

As in all professional situations, a trainer has a duty to exercise personal accountability and to act in a professionally competent fashion. This extends to making sure that they are working alongside presenters who are equally competent, especially if co-leading exercises. From a client-protection point of view, professional accountability would also require intervention if the trainer witnessed something in the course of a training session that was felt to be harmful to participants.

It is, of course, essential to have liability insurance to cover a whole range of professional activities. This should most certainly include workshop presentations and any training materials that are disseminated, in case these could also be relied upon to a participant's detriment. As in all cases, if a trainer is not sure whether the policy extends to workshop presentations, they should find this out before taking part.

* * *

6.3 What could happen to me if my client were to recognize herself in a published case study, even if heavily disguised (she left therapy before I could get her permission)?

The first point is that clients are not obliged to take part in educational exercises. The ethical basis of the therapeutic encounter is that it is in the client's best interests. A case study designed to assist in the training or continuing professional development (CPD) needs of other practitioners is not directly in the client's best interests, even though hopefully it will benefit other clients in the longer term. Although it is generous and altruistic of people to participate in education and research, there is no legal duty for them to do so. In rare circumstances, such as epidemiological medical research, it may be justified to use non-identifiable information about a client without permission. Clients receiving therapy in a teaching hospital environment may be somewhat more inclined to participate in education or research. Beyond this, client records should not be used for training or research without express consent. In other words, a client must be explicitly asked whether they are prepared to have their personal health information shared with others. As a matter of autonomy, it is the fundamental right of the individual to control who has access to information about them. The publication of an unauthorized case study is an infringement of the individual's autonomy and could be psychologically harmful. The counter-argument is that ongoing research and case studies in professional journals are vital to train new practitioners and to refine the skills of existing practitioners.

Professional guidelines in all healthcare professions recognize the need for lifelong learning and CPD. Healthcare professionals are being encouraged or required to participate in these initiatives to show that they are keeping up to date with current good practice. As such, there might be pressure on practitioners to publish, and this might tempt some practitioners to cut corners. This is both unethical and may potentially constitute a breach of client confidentiality. The defences to this might include that the case was of such educational interest that disclosure was warranted or that the case study was justified in the public interest (having made all reasonable attempts to maintain confidentiality). If working within an NHS Trust, any relevant protocols relating to case studies containing personal health information must be followed strictly.

Unfortunately, in this case, consent has not been sought. Although the client's details have been altered, she clearly has not been sufficiently well disguised. This is a problem within counselling and psychotherapy, where it may not be possible to alter too much personal information without distorting the case study. But for the reasons stated, it is unethical practice not to seek a client's permission. If the client had already left therapy before permission could be sought, the counsellor should have excluded this particular client's case and should have chosen one from whom consent could be obtained.

In terms of legal consequences, one possible outcome could be the client taking action for breach of confidence. A therapist has a duty of confidence towards the client arising from the special, confiding nature of the relationship, as an implied or express term of a legal contract, and also under data protection and human rights law. More likely, however, is a complaint brought against the offending therapist under their professional association's complaints procedure. The climate surrounding issues of client confidentiality has shifted away from an automatic assumption of the therapist's right to publish material for educational and training purposes and towards a much more specific protection for the rights of clients to continued anonymity. Guidelines from the General Medical Council, for example, refer to the need to obtain the 'express consent' of the patient for inclusion in a published case history or journal article. Anecdotal evidence points a number of situations where former students and clients have recognized themselves in case presentations made by therapists, and, no doubt, been also recognized by third parties. Where the material is in audio- or video-tape form, the ethical problems arising from client recognition and potential breach of confidentiality are even more apparent. As therapy training has expanded dramatically in the last decade, so the potential audience for training case vignettes and for video clips has grown proportionately in scale. In some cases, former clients have withdrawn their earlier consent for their inclusion in training videos and any unauthorized use of this material could potentially result in legal action.

* * *

6.4 My current client is in counselling for sexual problems, including indecent exposure – for which, incidentally, he has never been caught by the police. To my dismay, he now proudly tells me he has been accepted onto a local diploma in counselling course. Should I do something to alert the course tutors, as I feel strongly that future clients would be at risk?

Unfortunately, the recruitment policies of most counselling training organizations are insufficiently rigorous. Although police checks are made of public-sector and voluntary workers who will be in contact with children and vulnerable adults, most courses do not carry out even rudimentary checks on prospective students. The proliferation of counselling courses in recent years has led to concerns about the depth and quality of some counselling training. Ideally, courses should be more proactive in weeding out students who they think will not make good practitioners, on the grounds that they are too beset by their own personal problems to be able to help others effectively.

The main legal question here is whether the therapist should breach the client's confidentiality. This would probably be detrimental to the therapeutic relationship. The client may have an expectation that confidentiality will continue to be maintained because he has admitted that he has indecently exposed himself and the therapist has not reported him to the police up to this point in their therapeutic relationship.

Here, the practitioner does not have an absolute duty to breach confidentiality (as would be the case if the client identified himself as being involved in terrorist activities). Rather, the dilemma is whether to exercise the discretion to breach confidentiality. This requires the therapist to weigh up whether the possibility of actual risk to the public outweighs the client's right to confidentiality. Indecent exposure, while offensive to many, might be seen by some to lie at the lower end of a spectrum of sexual offences in terms of seriousness. Is it possible to predict with any degree of accuracy how much of a danger to the public and, indeed, to fellow students and potential clients this person poses? Might the therapist feel sufficiently optimistic with the way the counselling is proceeding to hope that the client will continue to make good progress and that the threat can be minimized by further therapy?

Is the questioner's dismay legitimate? A positive experience of counselling can act as the springboard to many people who then decide to pursue training in counselling. If counselling is helping the client's problem, should he not be given the opportunity to pursue a chosen field of study? Might it not be that the process of counselling training may give him further insight into his own problems?

One question to consider is whether any legal liability could arise if the therapist fails to disclose this information and the client then abused a fellow student or a member of the public. The issue of disclosure to protect third parties has already been discussed in the responses to Questions 2.7, 4.3 and 4.6. Might a therapist be sued if it were revealed that they knew about this behaviour but had not acted to alert the relevant authorities? The *Tarasoff* case, discussed above, raised a similar issue. There, a university counsellor failed to advise that one of his clients had threatened to kill his girlfriend. The dead girl's family successfully sued the university employing the counsellor for his failure to warn. Since this is a United States case, it is not legally binding on United Kingdom law, but it is helpful to look at the reasoning behind it. In the *Tarasoff* example, the threat of harm was most specific and targeted at a named individual. Thus, if the girl and the police had been warned in advance, there was a real possibility that significant, substantial harm could have been averted.

There would be stronger grounds for making the disclosure if the client had been arrested and convicted in the past for this offence. Police checks on students are now carried out as routine by many agencies providing placements in the voluntary sector, particularly where the client group includes children and vulnerable adults. Disclosure of past convictions would also be necessary for a counselling student wanting a job or a placement in the statutory sector. In fact, for a student with a past conviction for sexual offences even to *seek* employment or regular contact with children would constitute a further offence.

However, in this situation, in the absence of any proof beyond what the client has told the therapist (which may, of course, be inaccurate, exaggerated or even fabricated), there would seem less justification for telling the course tutors. Risk assessment is notoriously unreliable. The therapist may have a strong gut instinct that it is inappropriate for this client to work as a counsellor, as they feel that their future clients would be at risk, but upon what evidence is this based? At this stage, the student has only been accepted onto a diploma course, and he may, indeed, decide that he does not want to engage in professional practice at some later stage.

However, as in all situations, a therapist has discretion whether or not to disclose this information. Should the decision be to do so, disclosure should be restricted to the course tutors, as they are in the best position to prevent the harm from materializing. A decision to breach confidentiality has to be justified by the likelihood of averting harm. In other words, a therapist would *not* be entitled to broadcast this information in the local paper. Whenever a breach of confidentiality is contemplated, information should not be disclosed without having attempted to get the client to disclose this information themselves.

A further point to bear in mind is that, were the therapist to write a reference for this client, which expressed concern in detail, the client may conceivably have access to this under the Data Protection Act. Practice and policy seems to vary according to the training organization involved, but the principle of client or 'data subject' access to their files means that references may be disclosed to the individual. This may or may not be a factor in influencing the writing of such a communication. Should the client object to the information included in a reference or letter, a defence could be based on the grounds of 'qualified privilege'. This entitles information, which might otherwise be construed as being unfavourable or even defamatory, to be communicated by one person, with the appropriate authority, to another with a corresponding responsibility to receive it. The communication needs to be made 'without malice'. Practitioners have been cautious about using this as a means for reporting malpractice, misconduct or risk to others in the past, precisely because of the ambiguity and uncertainty surrounding the outcome. Nevertheless, it remains a valid method of passing on sensitive information in the public interest, if carried out in a responsible and fully professional manner. Once again, obtaining prior, accurate and informed legal advice would be a sensible precaution here.

* * *

6.5 As a supervisor, my approach is that I take clinical responsibility for my supervisee's therapeutic practice. Does it follow that I could be sued if they were found to be professionally negligent?

The benefits of supervision to effective practice have been well documented. Because counsellors and psychotherapists often work in private practice, supervision provides an opportunity to receive professional reassurance, mentoring, companionship and to learn from the practice wisdom of colleagues. Supervision also recognizes that a newly qualified practitioner needs to continue to develop and refine their practice. Supervision, as part of lifelong learning, facilitates the practitioner's professional and personal development and provides a useful safeguard against overzealous or misguided therapeutic practice. The role of supervisor is therefore extremely important and does have potential legal ramifications.

One legal aspect of the therapist-supervisor relationship relates to client consent. Not all practitioners tell their clients that they are themselves receiving supervision. This may because they do not want to seem inexperienced or because they regard supervision solely as a tool for their own personal and professional development. However, the expectation of confidentiality is such that therapists receiving supervision should disclose this fact to their clients. Specifically, clients have a right to know whether the specific details of their case will be discussed between the therapist and the supervisor and, if so, what rights to confidentiality they may expect in these circumstances, and whether the supervisor has any therapeutic obligations towards them.

The fact that clients' material is taken to supervision should be disclosed at the outset of therapy or even prior to its commencement. A practitioner who does not disclose this information to a patient is breaching the relationship of trust, which underpins the therapeutic encounter. Failure to disclose could conceivably constitute a breach of the practitioner's duty of confidentiality towards the client and might be considered as professional misconduct by the therapist's professional body.

From a broader perspective, the nature of the supervisory relationship means that a supervisor will, from time to time, become aware of cases with which the counsellor is experiencing some difficulty. For this reason, it is important to agree contractual lines of responsibility and mechanisms for accountability for all supervisory relationships. The supervisor may, for example, be bound by the terms of their contract with the relevant training organization, or with the placement agency, to report back any concerns about client welfare, or any questionable practice on the part of the supervisee.

Supervisors take their responsibilities very seriously, and, for some, this means adopting a stance of assuming clinical responsibility for the work of the supervisee. However, the term 'clinical responsibility' is somewhat of a loaded term. It introduces, but does not clearly resolve, the issue of the degree to which the supervisor is actually responsible, in a narrowly legal sense, for the mistakes or abusive practice of the therapist being supervised. One suggestive pointer in this direction comes from United States case law, where supervisors have been held to be liable for their supervisee's practice, for example where a counsellor started a sexual relationship with a current client.

However, United States case law, while of interest, may be of less direct relevance here than might be assumed. The concept applying there – of supervisor liability for counsellor malpractice – relates largely to certain state registration schemes, where the counsellor is permitted to practice only under direct and close supervision. This is in contrast with most arrangements for supervision of counselling and psychotherapy applying in the United Kingdom. Here, contact with a supervisor may be regular, on the basis of an hour and a half per month, or even more frequent than that, but the supervisor will often not have detailed knowledge of the clients being seen or may lack direct lines of contact with the specific agency concerned. In this sense, much counselling and psychotherapy supervision is carried out at arm's length. It depends a good deal on the therapist's candour in accurately disclosing the nature of their work, the issues and problems encountered, and also on the supervisor's skill in picking up problematic aspects of the work. Supervision could perhaps be more accurately described as a form of professional consultation. It does not normally involve the type of close scrutiny associated with line management responsibility, which is often a part of supervision in other allied professions, such as social work and nursing.

Whether or not the supervisor is liable for the work of their supervisee, and therefore could be sued, depends critically on the existence of a duty of care. If the courts hold that there is no duty of care in a certain professional relationship, the victim of negligence cannot sue for damages. The client would then have to bring an action on another basis, such as for breach of contract. As discussed in Questions 2.1, 2.5 and 2.8, the therapist clearly owes the client a duty of care. The supervisor also owes a corresponding duty of care to the therapist and should work to achieve at least the minimum standards expected of competently carrying out this role. A therapist could therefore, in theory at least, sue their *supervisor* for breach of this all-important duty of care.

Does the supervisor also owe a separate duty of care to the therapist's *client*? In other words, could the *client* sue the *supervisor* for failing to spot the therapist's ineffective, damaging or abusive work? To be honest, the answer to this question is not clear, and there are differing points of view on this between the authors themselves, as there are amongst other writers on this topic.

One view is that the supervisor could be held to owe such a duty of care to the client and could therefore be joined to the action brought by the client against the therapist concerned. It might be held by the court that the professional relationship between therapist and supervisor was sufficiently close that the latter should have had a close knowledge about the therapy being provided and should thus have been in a position to stop harm occurring to the client. In the absence of relevant case law, this remains a speculative possibility.

Another perspective is to focus on the employment relationship between supervisor and therapist as this can be a crucial factor in determining liability. Under the principle of vicarious liability, the employer is liable for the work carried out by staff in the course of their employment. A client with a grievance against a psychotherapist in the NHS, for example, would sue the NHS Trust, which employed that therapist. If the supervisor was also employed by the same NHS Trust, the Trust would also be vicariously liable for any inadequate supervision. To some extent, the concept of vicarious liability offers an umbrella of protection to therapists and supervisors, in that the employing organization is in the immediate line of fire and can provide legal representation for them. However, it has to be remembered that the same employer is also at liberty to bring later disciplinary proceedings against the staff concerned if there has been a major breach of accepted policy and practice, such as, for example, a failure to report a child who was clearly at risk of being abused.

A key question, in deciding whether supervisors are liable to clients, is the nature of their relationship to the therapist and agency concerned. Again, it is common practice for supervisors *not* to be directly employed by the therapist's own agency. In fact, this is often by deliberate choice on the practitioner's part, so that the supervisor brings a greater degree of professional distance and objectivity to their work. For example, a counsellor directly employed by a school might have a contract for monthly supervision with a supervisor who works quite separately in private practice. The supervisor, according to a strict reading of employment law, would not carry vicarious liability for the school counsellor if they failed to recognize and act on a young person's overtly suicidal ideation.

The issue of supervisor liability, in a narrow legal sense, has yet to be resolved by case law. In a wider professional and ethical sense, supervisors are eager to assume an overriding moral responsibility to safeguard and protect the welfare of clients to the best of their knowledge and ability. Whether this ethical duty corresponds with a specific legal duty of care is still uncertain. At the very least, however, supervisors should ensure that they are adequately covered by professional indemnity insurance for this aspect of their work in order to avoid any unpleasant surprises in the future.

CHAPTER 7

Professional activities and the law

Counsellors and psychotherapists are necessarily involved in a wide range of professional activities, each of which can carry a degree of uncertainty about legal requirements. These can include the professional responsibility for monitoring or reporting bad practice, the relationship of the law to professional complaints systems and to professional codes of ethics. Of continuing interest to many practitioners is the potential use of the law to regulate counselling as a profession. The final question responds to the question of how concerned professionals can gain access to appropriate legal advice as necessary.

7.1 Where do I stand if I come across bad practice in therapy within the NHS Trust where I work? How could I report such practice without running the risk of being disciplined or even dismissed?

This question highlights a dilemma in which many practitioners may find themselves. Most counsellors and psychotherapists faced with this situation would wish to take effective action and help to root out bad practice, should they come across it. However, to do so may arouse feelings of disloyalty towards colleagues and one's place of work. Moreover, many therapists will be aware that, in the past, people who have spoken out publicly, criticizing colleagues or their employers, have themselves been censured, marginalized and have even been subject to disciplinary proceedings or dismissal.

The attitude towards disclosing bad practice has been changing over a number of years. Whereas in the past, health carers perhaps closed ranks to protect underperforming, incompetent or ill colleagues, the NHS's commitment towards patient protection is now paramount. In this era of quality assurance and greater transparency, professional bodies and employing institutions now encourage – and, indeed, require in some circumstances – colleagues to report instances of misconduct or concerns about a colleague's health, particularly where this is putting patients at risk. For example, the British Association of Counselling and Psychotherapy's 'Ethical Framework' states that practitioners 'should raise their concerns with the practitioner concerned in the first instance, unless it is inappropriate to do so. If the matter cannot be resolved, they should review the grounds for their concern and the evidence available to them and, where appropriate, raise their concerns with the practitioner's manager, agency or professional body' (2002: 8).

In addition to making a disclosure to the relevant professional body, the terms of a therapist's NHS employment also require disclosures that are necessary to protect people who are at risk of harm. Since the Bristol tragedy, where an unacceptably high death rate for children undergoing heart surgery was discovered via professional whistleblowing activity, the government has introduced a scheme of clinical governance within the NHS. Clinical governance is defined as 'a framework through which NHS organizations are accountable for continuously improving the quality of their services and safeguarding high standards of care by creating an environment in which excellence in clinical care will flourish' ('A First Class Service: Quality in the new NHS': www.gov.uk/doh). Clinical governance requires:

- **commitment** from the top of the organization to put quality of care and patient safety at the top of the agenda
- **creation of a culture** in which quality of care and service to patients can flourish. The right culture is characterized by a shared passion for quality, by openness and respect, by support and by fairness. It is not a culture in which people are swift to blame, to find scapegoats or seek retribution
- **procedures and practices** which mean that people throughout the organization will know how well care is being provided, understand their contribution to the quality of care and can identify and act upon opportunities for improving quality and safety ('Building a Safer NHS': www.gov.uk/doh)

In recognition of the difficulties faced by them, the Public Interest Disclosure Act 1988 (PIDA) now gives some statutory protection towards whistleblowers. This includes mechanisms for whistleblowers to bring an action if they are subsequently dismissed or victimized as a result of a disclosure that is protected by the Act. The Act applies to people at work raising genuine concerns about crime, civil offences (including negligence, breach of contract, breach of administrative law), miscarriage of justice, danger to health and safety or the environment and the deliberate concealment of any of the above.

Under the Act, a disclosure in good faith to a manager or the employer will be protected, if the whistleblower has a reasonable suspicion that malpractice has occurred, is occurring or is likely to occur. This applies whether or not the information is confidential. The Act applies to every professional providing general medical services within the NHS and would apply to practitioners providing counselling services within the NHS. The usual employment law restrictions on minimum length of service and age do not apply. The Act does not currently extend to those who are self-employed or volunteers; so, if providing counselling services for the NHS on this basis, a therapist would not come within the terms of the Act.

Despite this shift, there are still constraints that need to be taken into account before making a disclosure about bad practice. It is most important to make sure that the facts are accurate and that any comments are justified and honest. The Act's protections apply only where the disclosure of bad practice has been made to the appropriate authority. This will vary from institution to institution. In the first instance, this may be the line manager, the Trust's chief executive or the institutions' risk manager. Every NHS Trust and health authority is now expected to have in place local policies and procedures that comply with the provisions of the Act. Reporting arrangements will also include a confidential reporting channel for staff who do not have confidence in making a report openly.

It is hoped that, once the appropriate authorities have been alerted to the problems, steps will be taken to ensure that the situation is appropriately dealt with. A concern would arise where, if having reported bad practice, the appropriate authorities failed to act on the problem. This would then put the therapist in the difficult position of deciding whether to widen disclosure to outside the institution, for example by writing an article or letter to the local or national press. Employers are entitled to expect that their employees will act within laid-down protocols for reporting internal problems. Taking a complaint further could be perceived as a breach of employer confidentiality and may lead to disciplinary proceedings. Again, the PIDA provides certain protections, provided that the disclosure is not made for personal gain. One of three preconditions also needs to be met. These are that the whistleblower:

- reasonably believed they would be victimized if they raised the matter internally or with a prescribed regulator
- reasonably believed a cover-up was likely and there was no prescribed regulator
- had already raised the matter internally or with a prescribed regulator

In deciding on the reasonableness of the disclosure, the tribunal will consider the identity of the person to whom it was made, the seriousness of the concern, whether the risk or danger remains and whether it breached a duty of confidence that the employer owed to a third party. This may be the case if the risk of harm related to one or more patients and the disclosure necessarily involved disclosing their identity. It needs to be remembered that, in addition to a professional duty of confidentiality, there may be a separate duty of confidentiality arising from a contract of employment.

However, a therapist's first professional duty is towards the safety of clients. This means ensuring not only their own competence but also being satisfied of the competence of colleagues. This is also an important risk-management issue. For issues of both patient safety and the avoidance of claims, bad practice needs to be rooted out before it results in adverse incidents, causing harm to patients and potential liability for the Trust. The approach to rooting out bad practice is therefore one of prevention and learning from mistakes. The emphasis is on developing a reporting culture, with root-cause analysis of adverse events, including specified near-misses. This culture requires thinking about systems and making learning effective so that risk and recurrence are reduced, with change taking place within the organization concerned (locally) and at national level (NHS-wide).

Clearly, while the above discussion draws on NHS policy and practice, the key points made will also apply more generally to other employment contexts in both the public and private sectors. Provided disclosure is limited in light of the above advice, a therapist should be protected from personal censure or disciplinary action. In any such a case, advice should nonetheless be sought from the therapist's professional body and insurers before proceeding with a whistleblowing initiative.

* * *

7.2 What is the legal protection provided to a counsellor or psychotherapist in following their professional code of ethics? Would this be sufficient defence in a legal dispute over standards if this ever came to court?

The first point to note is that, while there may be other positive reasons to do so, there is no specific legal protection in following a professional code of ethics. Membership of a professional body will explicitly or implicitly require a commitment to upholding that body's code of ethics. Although broadly similar, legal responsibilities are not identical to ethical responsibilities. Accordingly, there may be situations where the advice given in a code of ethics is at variance with the strict position in law.

Most codes of ethics are a synthesis of minimal legal requirements and statements of ethical ideals. These are backed up with professional statements, which represent the shared political and economic ideals of that particular group. Codes are often couched in negative terms, listing obvious prohibitions (don't breach client confidentiality, don't have abusive relationships with clients etc.). They do not usually provide detailed guidance on how the code should be applied in complex situations or how a practitioner should act when duties seemingly conflict (for example what to do when the duty to respect a client's privacy clashes with the perceived need to protect third parties from harm).

In order to be effective and relevant, codes need to be updated from time to time to reflect current best practice as well as changes in the law and professional policy. An obvious problem in the United Kingdom is that numerous registering bodies exist, each of which has its own codes of ethics. Whereas some registering bodies have produced excellent, relevant documents, other codes of ethics are more tokenistic and provide sketchy, and sometimes outdated, advice. It goes without saying, that if a code of ethics contains inaccurate or incomplete legal advice, this is not going to provide a practitioner with a sound basis for acting within the law.

So to what extent do codes provide a therapist with a basis for legal practice? The emphasis of most codes is on the therapist's duties in relation to clients, other practitioners, the counselling and psychotherapy professions and society as a whole. In terms of duties towards clients, codes focus mainly on duties relating to respecting autonomy, benefiting and not harming clients, and treating all clients fairly and with respect for difference. These ethical responsibilities mirror the practitioner's legal responsibilities discussed in this book, in terms of gaining informed consent, respecting privacy and confidentiality, treating a client with due care and skill, and acting in a non-discriminatory manner.

As seen in previous questions, a court, in deciding whether a therapist has acted unlawfully, will take evidence from expert witnesses as to the prevailing professional standards. Practitioners, broadly speaking, are required to work within practices accepted as proper by a responsible body of counselling opinion. It follows that a counsellor or psychotherapist, who is working within the duties set out by their professional body, ought to satisfy this professional-friendly standard of competence.

Codes of ethics stress the requirement of a professional to be technically competent as well as ethically accountable. If we consider the main legal actions likely to be brought against a counsellor – namely an action in negligence, breach of contract or battery – a practitioner who is strictly adhering to the tenets of their duty-based code ought to be able to avoid legal complaint.

How far does adherence to a particular code provide a specific defence for a legal action? The role of codes in protecting practitioners is most easily understood in relation to negligence and the standard of care required by a professional. Reliance on codes of ethics certainly provides preliminary evidence that the counsellor was acting within a standard accepted as proper by a responsible body of professional opinion (that is according to the *Bolam* test). Specific allegations of wrongdoing would have to be decided by the court on the basis of the individual facts of the case. For legal purposes, advice contained in professional guidelines could be said to represent prima facie evidence of acceptable current practice. But codes of ethics rarely cover all eventualities. The therapist will still have to make finely nuanced decisions about how to apply the spirit of the code, where it is not obvious how to proceed.

It is hoped that there will be very few instances where acting ethically conflicts with a therapist's legal position. A possible example might be where a therapist is required to produce case records but is reluctant to do so because this would breach the client's confidentiality. In such a situation, one would expect a court to show sensitivity to the need for confidentiality within professional therapist-client relationships. A refusal to disclose information based on an interpretation of the code's insistence that therapists respect their clients' privacy and confidentiality will certainly be taken into account by the court but might, nonetheless, be ultimately overridden.

Ultimately, every practitioner is accountable for their own actions. A therapist might have to decide whether a departure from norms of accepted practice is justified in the particular case. The therapist would also need to be prepared to defend that decision, if necessary, both before a court and before their professional body, should a complaint be made. A reassuring feature of voluntary self-regulation is that it allows for a wide diversity in counselling and psychotherapy techniques, leading to a considerable diversity of professional views and approaches. The test for negligence, looked at from another perspective, is that a counsellor or psychotherapist will only be negligent if they are acting in a way which no reasonable practitioner would have acted. The current regulatory framework, therefore, allows a practitioner a wide scope of practice. Remember, too, that it is not acting negligently merely to pursue a minority view, provided that it is a view held by a responsible body of professional opinion.

What if a therapist's practice deviates from all accepted wisdom? The law, as discussed earlier, would not hold a practitioner negligent merely for holding a minority view, provided that this was supported by a professional body of opinion. While this would be the case for issues of technical competence, a court would look less favourably on a practitioner who decided unilaterally that they were exempt from certain parts of the code of ethics, for example those prohibiting sexual relationships with clients.

Codes of ethics offer broad, general advice, not a blueprint for action. As an example, a therapist may feel that, in satisfying the duty to promote the client's autonomy in the long term, it is justified to use deception. The court would have to rely on expert evidence to decide whether this was appropriate in the particular case. Although it is good advice to follow the provisions of a professional code, it would be unwise to treat it as providing definitive answers to all the problems that may be faced. Finally, a professional code of ethics is only one of a raft of services provided by most regulatory bodies, most of which also offer telephone advice when practitioners encounter problems. It is important that detailed records are kept of any conversations had with a professional body in relation to a difficult case, as any advice they give may also be called in evidence in an attempt to judge the reasonableness of a therapist's conduct.

* * *

7.3 What can I do as a therapist if I find out that my client, or a colleague, is spreading libel or slander about me?

Although most people understand libel and slander under the collective notion of 'bad-mouthing', it is important to distinguish these separate aspects of defamation. Defamation is written or spoken injury to a person's reputation. A defamation action is to protect a person's reputation. Both slander and libel are concerned with words constituting an attack on the integrity of an individual, which would lead a right-thinking person to think less of them as a result. Whereas slander refers to the spoken word, libel involves an attack in writing. This could involve a newspaper or magazine article, or something published on the Internet.

If a therapist has been libelled or slandered, there are several options. What is decided will obviously depend largely on how seriously the allegation is taken and how harmful it is thought to be to the therapist's personal and professional reputation. A one-off slander made by a client (Mrs X told Mrs Y that her counsellor was 'woolly and totally unreliable') may be considerably less troubling than an inflammatory article published by a critical colleague in the local press ('Beware: local counsellor uses discredited technique'). As different responses may be available in each case, we will consider defamation by a client and by a colleague separately.

If a therapist finds out that a client has maligned them, one view might be that the defamation is trifling and not worth pursuing through legal channels. However, it is still worth considering what has prompted their discontent. One way of doing this is to confront the client and get to the root of their concerns. It may be that the defamation has arisen out of a misunderstanding, which ideally can be resolved at an informal level. Of course, it is possible that the complaint has come from a former client who does not wish to discuss the matter face to face.

Complaints of any sort are likely to provoke a defensive and angry reaction, but it should be borne in mind that client dissatisfaction can be seen as a positive opportunity to reflect on working practices and to consider changes where necessary. According to the BACP's guidance, if something has gone wrong, clients should be reminded of the existence of the professional conduct procedures that will be open to them, as well as making them aware of any other applicable complaints or disciplinary procedures. Where a therapist feels that they have acted in accordance with good practice but the client disagrees, the client might be encouraged to seek a second opinion, where this is appropriate.

If, however, a client is repeatedly slandering a therapist, or has written something libellous, this may be felt to pose a sufficient threat to integrity and professional livelihood that the therapist is compelled to take legal action. Before embarking on this route, it is important to be aware that legal aid is not available for libel trials and that taking someone to court is likely to be an emotionally and financially draining business. Remember, too, that a statement can be defamatory but true. Also, a judge sitting with a jury decides most defamation cases. Juries have been known to arrive at unpredictable verdicts, when deciding if someone's reputation has been damaged.

In bringing a defamation action, the claimant must show that defamatory words (in the relevant and particular context) were published (that is somebody other than the claimant and the defendant saw the words) and that they caused damage to reputation. The claimant must have a reputation that can be damaged. A defendant may, by way of answer, establish that one of the above elements was not present, that the defamatory words are true (a defence to an action) or that some other reason (such as legitimate public interest) protects the publication in law. A counsellor seeking to rebut such an allegation must be careful to avoid defaming the client in turn ('Mrs X would say that – she's totally neurotic...'). Defamation is a highly specialized area of law, and, if this route is pursued, advice should certainly be sought from lawyers with specialist knowledge in this area. Unless a therapist's entire professional livelihood hangs in the balance, a defamation action will rarely be worthwhile. Remember, though, that a skilfully worded letter threatening legal action may be sufficient to prevent further defamation.

If it is discovered that a colleague has been defaming the therapist, the options, as above, include confronting that person to attempt to reach an amicable agreement, with provision for an appropriate retraction if necessary. In addition, if the colleague is a member of the same professional body or belongs to another credible registering organization, it may be possible to make a professional complaint about them. As discussed in Question 7.1, therapists, like other health professionals, are expected to report bad practice when they come across it. Properly understood, this does not interfere with the notion of professional etiquette, specifically the currently somewhat discredited duty not to denigrate colleagues. Most codes of ethics stress the importance of maintaining respect for the counselling profession as a whole, and the importance of fostering good working relationships with colleagues. The BACP's code states:

> Practitioners must not undermine a colleague's relationships with clients by making unjustified or unsustainable comments. (BACP, 2002: 9)

As with an action for defamation, there is an inbuilt qualifier that it may be legitimate to criticise a colleague if there is justification for doing so, that is where the comments are justified and sustainable. As above, it is worth considering whether a professional disciplinary action will draw more attention to oneself than the situation merits, since any action is likely to put a therapist's own professional practice under close scrutiny. Nonetheless, if defamed by a colleague, it might be felt that the consequences are more damaging than being defamed by a client and that it is worth taking action to clear one's name. This needs to be balanced against the fact that, once a person has been defamed, the clock cannot be turned back (although it may be possible to insist that a retraction or apology be published). The damages, which may be awarded if successful, may be little compensation for the unfavourable press coverage that any such action might attract.

* * *

7.4 I am starting up a counselling service via email. Are there any legal issues I need to be aware of?

A number of counselling organizations and individual practitioners have introduced, or are considering introducing, online counselling. In addition to generalized information about services and counselling, online counselling includes counselling provided by email and/or the use of Internet relay chat (IRC), where the counsellor and client are online simultaneously so that a virtual dialogue is created. An obvious benefit of online counselling is that it facilitates service provision to a broader range of clients, including those who find it difficult to access face-to-face counselling. Currently, the use of online counselling is under-researched, and, as with the introduction of any innovative therapy, practitioners need to be particularly aware of potential legal and ethical pitfalls.

The prime concern is whether online counselling is able to offer a safe, quality service. Before considering the specific legal issues raised by online counselling, counsellors should consider how the law of negligence, previously discussed, might be applied to this form of working. Broadly speaking, the counsellor has a professional duty to ensure that the benefits of using this form of counselling outweigh any risks and limitations. Risks inherent in online service provision need to be anticipated and catered for so that the likelihood of harm is minimized.

Careful pre-assessment would be required so that online counselling is only offered in appropriate cases. Clients, for example, with learning disabilities, or who may require psychiatric referral, might be unsuitable for this sort of working relationship. Clients need to be made fully aware of the limitations and potential difficulties in this form of working so that they can decide whether they wish to pursue online counselling rather than a traditional approach. Therapists need to consider whether online consent is possible or whether a separate written form should be signed. Particular concern needs to be exercised when working with minors or other vulnerable groups, since the laws governing the treatment of minors and the ability of others to provide proxy consent varies from jurisdiction to jurisdiction.

As with face-to-face counselling, competence to offer online services will be a key issue. As in all spheres, practitioners are accountable for their actions. Competence to deliver face-to-face counselling does not automatically imply competence to deliver online counselling. The challenges posed by online working require specialized training and supervision, and it is highly unlikely that this would be a suitable medium for a novice practitioner. Moreover, setting up an online service is likely to require a considerable financial and time investment. At the present time, this form of working may be more appropriate to an organization than an individual, since organizations tend to be better resourced and have access to necessary IT expertise.

The BACP identifies the following additional areas of competence required by a practitioner working online:

- the shift from verbal to written communication skills
- the importance and difficulties of building and maintaining adequate therapeutic relationships online
- the importance of greater clarification than in face-to-face work so that misunderstandings do not occur
- assessment issues and skills when working online, for example establishing the suitability of counselling for the issues at hand and for the

individual concerned and in terms of the physical and transactional limitations of online provision

- appreciation of appropriate administrative practices, for example legal obligations, data storage
- adequate knowledge of technical questions relating to security, privacy etc.

Although there is no United Kingdom case law in this area as yet, a court, if considering whether a counsellor had been negligent in the provision of online service, would look to professional guidelines as evidence of what would be required of a 'reasonably competent' practitioner in this area.

Because of the nature of online counselling, the therapist must make sure that the terms of the contract are properly understood by a prospective client. In addition to the usual features of a counselling contract, the following factors need to be dealt with:

- **Time boundaries**: how long the counsellor will take to read and respond to emails. Mention must be made of availability to the client. Counsellors contemplating an email service should be careful to explain that this does not mean they are available 24 hours a day.
- **Fees and fee structure**: whether fees will be charged by the hour, by the message, how clients can pay using a secure online billing service, what exchange rate will apply in the case of international clients.
- **Law of contract**: determining which country's laws will apply in the event of dispute, and what regulatory frameworks will apply. This is vital because the laws and regulations governing counselling practice vary from jurisdiction to jurisdiction.
- **Alternative means of communication**: this is essential in case either party's computer hardware or software breaks down, as well as the steps that will be taken in the event of a technical breakdown to restore online service. As with a face-to-face relationship, a contact number should be given for emergencies.
- **Confidentiality and data protection**: steps that will be taken to minimize risks during transmission, and unauthorized access, for example by Internet service providers.

Another issue with potential legal consequences is referral. It may be that, even if a counselling relationship has been started online, it becomes obvious that this is not the optimal way of working with a particular client. At this point, the practitioner may need to be able to make an appropriate referral. This may present difficulties when working with international clients, since referrals across geographical boundaries may be difficult and referral practices vary from country to country. A possible solution would be to request a local medical contact before commencing therapy.

A counsellor or psychotherapist relying on online technology must take steps to maintain any computer equipment and systems being used. In particular, steps must be taken to ensure that unauthorized users do not have access to the data, that the integrity of data is preserved and that a system recovers completely and rapidly from unanticipated disruptions. To provide an optimal service, practitioners should only offer this type of counselling if they have up-to-date hardware and software and the ability to replace or repair equipment quickly. Counsellors should also install anti-virus software to avoid the inadvertent transmission of viruses to clients.

In terms of confidentiality, online services provide greater risks than face-to-face counselling. Counsellors and clients must be aware of the possibility of interception of confidential data by a third party. Accordingly, counsellors will need to be familiar with additional mechanisms to protect client confidentiality. These include encryption, the use of passwords and the giving of advice on how to delete traces of their email/Internet usage. Counsellors should also warn clients about the danger of using, for example, a work computer, given that many employers routinely access their employee's emails. Again, different countries have different regulations governing third-party access to sensitive email information, which allows police and other national agencies to search and intercept emails in varying situations.

Therapists should note that the Data Protection Act 1998 applies to all computerized records. The counsellor should tell the client in advance of therapy how their data will be processed, for what purposes the information will be used (including training and research purposes) whether any third party would have access to the data (for example for the purposes of supervision). Clients should also be informed as to what security mechanisms are in place to secure their personal data, including the use and security of any back-up or printed-off copies of the information. Finally, practitioners should make sure that they carry adequate professional indemnity insurance to cover working in this new medium.

* * *

7.5 I have been the subject of a complaint by my professional association, and I feel that I have been unfairly treated in the process. I depend upon my counselling practice for my livelihood, so this is very important to me. How do I go about clearing my name?

Most professional bodies strive hard to achieve a balance between protecting members of the public from harm and protecting practitioners from vexatious, frivolous or inappropriate complaints. In order to ensure that a claim has merit, most professional bodies operate a vetting procedure for complaints, weeding out unsubstantiated complaints. Usually, this involves prior consideration by a Preliminary Investigating Committee (PIC), the purpose of which is to ensure that, by the time a case proceeds to the Professional Conduct Committee (PCC), the regulatory body will feel that there is at least a case to answer.

As with cases heard in a court of law, most regulatory bodies operate within a quasi-legal format, with evidence being presented by both sides to the complaint, with an opportunity to cross-examine witnesses. Each case will be decided on its own merits, and both parties usually have the opportunity to be legally represented. All professional bodies strive to be impartial and professional in their deliberations. Having a strong lay presence on any disciplinary panel enhances impartiality.

However, the adversarial nature of these hearings though means that, in any given case, the professional body will arrive at a decision which either the complainant or the defendant might believe to be wrong. It is natural to be concerned that a complaint, whatever its outcome, will have an adverse effect on one's practice. If the complaint has resulted in suspension or erasure from the professional register, this may have implications for whether a therapist feels able to continue in practice.

If someone feels that they have been unfairly treated, a number of courses of action are open to them. In the first instance, the appeals procedures operated by the professional body should be used. They (or their legal representatives) should check the wording of their professional guidance very carefully, as many professional bodies limit appeals to cases where there have been procedural irregularities, not merely where the complainant disputes the outcome of a hearing and wants another opportunity to clear their name.

Ultimately, the public nature of the disciplinary function of a professional body means that its verdicts may be subject to what is known in law as 'judicial review'. This is a branch of public law and may provide remedies where an individual has been treated unfairly by a public body. Bringing an action for judicial review is, in lay terms, an allegation that the professional body has reached a decision which no reasonable public body could have arrived at on the evidence. Probably the remedy that would be most applicable would be an order to quash the original verdict. Another factor to consider here is the impact of the Human Rights Act 1998. Professional associations have had to revise their disciplinary procedures, where there was potential conflict with Article 6 of the Act, namely the right to a fair trial. Any situation where there is a significant breach of natural justice, for example where an investigator of the original complaint also acted as part of the decision-making body imposing a sanction, would arguably be in breach of the therapist's human rights on this basis.

Bringing such an action against a professional association is subject to all the usual provisos about initiating any form of legal action. While it may be felt that one's livelihood is at stake, it is important to be aware of the enormous burden of undertaking a legal action to clear one's name. Before embarking upon litigation, it needs to be reckoned that a court action can drag on over many years, with the associated mental and financial toll. Because of this, it is vital to think rationally about how far a complaint is likely to affect professional practice and how much the desire to set the record straight is an angry response to having been the subject of a complaint.

If the appeal against the decision of the professional body is successful, what might be considered is drafting a summary of complaint (maintaining client confidentiality) and giving this to existing clients. Theoretically, this could be done in any event, setting out the nature of the complaint and the reasons why the body's findings are rejected. As with initiating an action for defamation, however, it needs to be asked whether this is blowing the issue out of proportion. It may be that many clients are more sympathetic to the therapist than one thinks and will continue to consult, even if a professional body has issued a censure. As has been mentioned many times already in this and other responses to questions, most complaints arise from poor communication. It may well be that being open with existing clients will work in the therapist's favour and that making it clear that the therapist will happily answer any queries or concerns they have about the case will allay their concerns.

* * *

7.6 When is the government going to regulate counselling and psychotherapy to protect clients from unqualified and dangerous practitioners?

Counselling and psychotherapy are currently voluntarily self-regulated professions. This means that the professional bodies responsible for regulating counselling and psychotherapy are free to determine what they consider to be requisite levels of training, to set their own professional standards and to deal with complaints as they see fit. Because there is not a single, overarching regulatory body, the current system allows many registering bodies to co-exist. Although many smaller organizations have now come together under the aegis of the British Association for Counselling and Psychotherapy (which merged the previous registers of the United Kingdom Council for Psychotherapy and the British Association for Counselling), splinter organizations still operate, all offering 'professional training' leading to 'professional qualifications'.

In terms of public safety, the drawback of voluntary self-regulation is that in the United Kingdom there exists a common-law freedom to practise. This means that any person is free to practise any profession which is not subject to protected title. While, therefore, it is unlawful and a criminal offence to describe oneself as doctor, nurse, optician, dentist, osteopath (or a member of any other statutorily regulated health profession that has protection of title) unless duly registered as such, anyone can call themselves a counsellor or psychotherapist. This, effectively, allows a therapist with little or no training to set up a counselling practice, subject only to market forces (whereby 'good' practitioners will supposedly flourish and 'bad' practitioners flounder, since dissatisfied clients will not return) and general legal requirements to protect others from harm. A voluntarily operated system of regulation offers considerable professional autonomy to individual practitioners but may inadequately protect potential clients from harm.

There have been several initiatives to introduce statutory regulation over the last few years, the most successful of which has been Lord Alderdice's bill in the House of Lords to regulate psychotherapy. While statutory self-regulation (SSR) may offer more effective safeguards to the public, practitioners should realize that voluntary self-regulation (VSR) and SSR share many of the same features, and that effective VSR can be equally able or unable to protect clients.

Both VSR and SSR are based on the existence, and maintenance by a professional body, of a register of duly qualified practitioners. Practitioners must have graduated from a training school that is recognized by the professional body as offering a suitable education. Clearly, within a single regulatory structure, it is easier to ensure consistency of high standards of training. Membership of both voluntary and statutory professional bodies requires that practitioners will work within a code of ethics and agree to be bound by the body's professional disciplinary mechanisms. A finding of serious professional misconduct may result in the practitioner's name being suspended or erased from the professional register.

SSR is not conferred by the government but sought by the profession itself. Whereas some practitioners view SSR as a right, it is in fact, a privilege. Being given professional status may change the way that the public and other stakeholders feel about an occupational group. Many practitioners feel that SSR confers legitimacy on a therapy. It is certainly the case that SSR can lead to a higher public profile. SSR may also assure doctors that counsellors are properly qualified, making them more confident about referring their patients to counsellors or employing counsellors within their practice.

The government will only intervene to recommend SSR for a therapy if that therapy is capable of causing serious harm, if practised by unskilled people. The transition from VSR to SSR happens when the government is persuaded that the profession in question has achieved professional maturity, demonstrating high standards of effective voluntary self-regulation. A pre-requisite of SSR is that different voices within the profession have united, or are in the process of coming together under a single umbrella, for the purposes of regulation. SSR is only possible when the profession is able to determine its scope of practice and can determine what is required for competent practice.

The difficulty of regulating counselling and psychotherapy by statute is that it is hard, if not impossible, to decide what level and types of therapeutic practice ought to be so regulated. There is a huge diversity within counselling and psychotherapy. Training varies from short courses put on by private trainers lasting a few weekends to externally accredited courses requiring several years' intensive study. Each course may entitle a graduate to use the term 'counsellor' or 'psychotherapist', but this of itself does not ensure that the practitioners are equally competent. Further logistical problems exist in protecting 'counselling' as a title, since so many professional groups (such as teachers or nurses) are engaged in using counselling skills in one form or other.

The key aim of any system of regulation is to protect the public from harm. Ideally, public protection is secured both through high standards of training and education and, also, through the existence of robust disciplinary procedures to censure professionals who fall below the standards required of a competent practitioner. It is widely assumed that SSR would provide stronger protections in this regard, by virtue of the fact that a person who was not qualified could no longer describe themselves as a counsellor or psychotherapist. Furthermore, in the event of suspension or erasure from the list of registered practitioners, a therapist would effectively be unable to practise.

It is vital to remember, though, that SSR is not a panacea. The existence of statutory regulation does not guarantee good practice, as indicated by the mass murders committed by GP Harold Shipman and the serious crimes carried out by nurse Beverley Allitt. The therapeutic relationship is, for the most part, carried out in private, behind closed doors. The practitioner, in possession of much personal information about the client, is in a position of considerable trust. Many clients may be emotionally vulnerable and in a state of distress. The onus is entirely on the therapist to act professionally and not to abuse the relationship of trust. This is the case whether the profession is statutorily or voluntarily regulated. Every profession has its share of bad apples, and counselling and psychotherapy are no exception. Even if there were much better vetting systems in place to weed out unsuitable counselling and psychotherapy students, it could still be extremely difficult to deter or detect a deviant practitioner.

The issue of VSR versus SSR is particularly relevant for therapies in which a significant proportion of its members work in private practice. Unlike working within the NHS or another institution, private practice lacks many of the safeguards necessary for client protection. Within the NHS, health professionals are subject to clinical governance, risk assessment, regular appraisal and are required to undertake continuing professional development. Practitioners working in the NHS are able to draw on the expertise of a multi-disciplinary team and practise within an evidence-based culture. A lone private practitioner could work in an entirely unsupervised manner. It may also be harder for a counsellor or psychotherapist working in isolation to be objective about their performance, as well as it being harder to keep up to date with current research and developments.

Aware of the dangers posed by unregulated private practice, the government has provided some alternative routes for health professions that are actively pursuing statutory regulation. In addition to the route of autonomous SSR, there is also the possibility of joining the recently configured Health Professions Council, which replaces the previous Council for Professions Supplementary to Medicine. This allows a number of health professions, currently including chiropody, physiotherapy and music therapy, to be united under a joint regulatory scheme. This regulatory approach is thought to be appropriate for smaller professions, whose membership is too small to bear the costs of SSR or for whom this level of client protection is felt to be sufficient.

* * *

7.7 Is there any way of getting good legal advice cheaply or even for free?

As with most professions, you pay for what you get, and quality legal services are expensive. It is, of course, worth bearing in mind that, if operating a business, some or all legal expenses can be set off against income. The amount may vary depending on whether the therapist is operating in sole private practice, as part of a partnership or has set up a limited company.

A professional body may also be a useful source of legal advice, particularly advice pertaining to professional practice. If a therapist has a separate trade union membership, or the professional body operates separately as a trade union, this is another source of useful information about the law. A drawback of approaching a professional body is that they will probably be reluctant to offer hypothetical advice, especially if they may be involved in the issue in question from a professional disciplinary point of view. Legal advice is also available from the Citizens Advice Bureau (see the local telephone book for the nearest office). It is hoped that a practitioner whose practice is soundly based on a good working knowledge of professional ethics and law will avoid complaints or litigation from clients. However, if legal services are required, always look for specialized practitioners rather than generalists.

Many therapists are somewhat anxious about the law and concerned about how to gain access to prompt accurate legal advice, should this prove to be necessary. Worries about cost can also be a major factor here. There are ways of gaining access to legal advice at low cost, or even for free, but each route carries with it some disadvantages and some necessary words of warning. Of course, the type of legal advice needed will vary considerably according to the nature of the legal action being considered. For example, a therapist seeking to be reimbursed by a client for the non-payment of fees can bring an action via the small claims court, where no legal representation is necessary. There are a number of websites and helpful sources of advice available (see the response to Question 2.3 for more detail on this procedure).

Other therapists may be concerned to gain legal advice on how best to respond to a complaint brought under the scope of their professional association. Alternatively, they may wish to bring more ambitious legal action in the form of a judicial review of a policy decision affecting them in an adverse way. Differing forms of legal action may involve varying levels of legal cost, and this needs to be taken into account at an early stage.

There are a number of ways of securing free legal advice. Where the therapist is employed, their employer should be able to provide legal advice via the solicitors acting for the agency. In large organizations, such as NHS Trusts or social services departments, there will normally be a legal section with some level of expertise in dealing with issues. This will also have useful contacts for getting more specialized representation, by barristers or by lawyers specializing, for example, in professional negligence or child abuse cases.

Therapists may be able to get legal advice from their own professional association. These increasingly employ staff with a legal background who have developed expertise in dealing with issues common to the association's membership, such as court-ordered access to client records. There is also informed coverage of legal issues to be found via going through back numbers of professional journals, on key issues such as reporting child abuse, the legal liability of supervisors and responding to requests by solicitors for case records.

Access to legal advice is normally provided by taking out professional indemnity insurance cover or via membership of a professional protection society, often via a telephone helpline. One problem with generic legal advice helplines, however, is that the legal advisor may not necessarily be that well informed about the specific nature of the therapist's ethical and professional concerns. The latter's response may be couched in terms of general legal principles rather than addressing a very specific concern related to a particular work setting, such as counselling children under 16 in a school. A current limitation of some professional indemnity insurance cover is that, apart from providing legal advice, the policy may not cover the cost of legal representation where the therapist is not an actual 'party to the case'. One instance of this is where therapists are seeking to resist demands to surrender sensitive client records under the legal process of disclosure. Technically, the therapist is not deemed to be an interested party to the case and may not therefore be able to have the costs of obtaining the legal services of a lawyer to represent their case for non-disclosure to the court.

Apart from the routes to legal advice suggested above, there are ways which are probably more familiar to therapists, in the sense that these are already fairly widely known to the public. Some access to legal advice comes as standard with home and domestic insurance cover, in addition to the more specific professional insurance referred to above. Legal advice can be obtained from trade unions, particularly where it relates to employment, as in the case of a counselling lecturer experiencing harassment from a current or past student on a course. Law centres and Citizens Advice Bureau may provide free initial legal advice. Many lawyers will provide a free first session so that an assessment can be made of the issues at stake and the likely cost of proceeding with a case. However, one point to bear in mind is that it may be important to use a solicitor with a specialist understanding of the professional and therapeutic issues at hand rather than a generalist who may be less familiar with issues of counselling confidentiality, data protection or professional negligence. Some law firms do specialise in these areas, and their details can be obtained from the Law Society or via other professional networks.

Another route for getting legal advice and representation is through using a conditional fee arrangement. Usually known as 'no win, no fee', this approach is increasingly replacing legal aid for claimants. Here, the lawyer can choose to take on a case for the client, who does not have to pay costs or damages if the case fails in court. If the case is won, the lawyer claims a higher fee. Clearly, the estimated chances for winning the case are a central factor here. High-risk cases, such as medical negligence, are likely to incur substantial costs in their preparation, through using reports by expert witnesses. In this situation, it is possible to take out an insurance policy to cover the legal costs and damages, should the case be lost. This route may also involve an initial charge by the solicitor to assess the merits of the case before deciding whether or not to take on the case.

A further option for therapists, though not one for the faint-hearted, would be to go it alone. Some key cases have actually been fought and won in the United Kingdom by therapists with partners or relatives who had legal training. One of the authors successfully acted for a partner and won a significant ruling clarifying the rights of the litigant to receive legal support in this respect.

One possibility is for the therapist to act as a 'litigant in person', by seeking to represent themselves in court. This could be with the support of a friend and advisor, acting as a 'McKenzie friend', or informal supporter, in the courtroom. This stance of acting as a litigant in person is, perhaps not surprisingly, not at all popular with the legal profession, with litigants being referred to variously as 'LIPs', 'lippies' or even 'loonies in person'. The numbers of those wanting to bring their own case or defend themselves in person are rising, even though the chances of success are very low. However, there have been some notable successes. Dave Morris and Helen Steel made a very effective defence against libel charges brought against them by McDonalds, the fast food chain, in what became the longest-running court case in English legal history. Frank Cunningham won damages of £325,000 at the court of appeal, against the combined forces of a QC, barrister and two solicitors in a medical negligence case. Keith Callan, imprisoned for causing serious injuries to his partner's daughter, studied neurology in detail in prison and effectively challenged the medical evidence underpinning his conviction, thus leading to his release. Michael Randle and Pat Pottle, charged with illegally aiding the escape from prison of the spy George Blake, won their acquittal from criminal charges after conducting their own defence in court, without reliance on lawyers.

Therapists may be involved in somewhat less high-profile cases but may still be looking for low-cost legal advice. If not prepared to act as a litigant in person, some legal advice and representation might be obtained by what used to be called 'pro bono' sources. (This derives from the Latin *pro bono publico*, that is 'for the public good', and is referred to as 'law for free' since the Woolfe reforms.) There are a number of sources providing free legal representation, including the services of QCs, such as the Bar Pro Bono Unit, Free Representation Unit, and Solicitors' Pro Bono Group (see Resources section for details). Some university law departments also provide legal surgeries.

At the end of the day, a therapist may be able to get legal advice and representation from a range of sources, ranging from free to low-cost and to the moderately, or even very, expensive. Given a degree of ingenuity and persistence, there is probably as much chance of a therapist obtaining access to free legal advice as there is a for a lawyer to gain access to free therapy, assuming that both parties know exactly where to look and know how to evaluate what is on offer.

Resources

Further reading

The following books and articles provide coverage of the main areas likely to be of interest to therapists, with Jenkins (1997) as the main overall introduction to therapy and the law. Additional coverage can be found in BACP publications, and in Bond's work (1998, 2000, 2001). Stone (1996, 2002) covers ethical and legal aspects of complementary and alternative therapy, which have many parallels with counselling and psychotherapy. More specialized coverage of particular topics can be found by contacting the organizations or websites listed below.

Bond T (1998) Counselling: Confidentiality and the Law. Rugby: British Association for Counselling and Psychotherapy.

Bond T (2000) Standards and Ethics for Counselling in Action (second edition). London: Sage.

Bond T, Higgins RA, Jamieson A (2001) Confidentiality: Counselling, Psychotherapy and the Law in Scotland. Rugby: British Association for Counselling and Psychotherapy.

Brandon S, Boakes J, Glaser D, Green R (1997) Recovered memories of childhood sexual abuse: implications for clinical practice. British Journal of Psychiatry 172: 296-307.

British Association for Counselling and Psychotherapy (2002) Ethical Framework for Good Practice in Counselling and Psychotherapy. Rugby: British Association for Counselling and Psychotherapy.

British Psychological Society (1995) Recovered Memories. Leicester: BPS.

Daniels D, Jenkins P (2000) Therapy with Children: Children's Rights, Confidentiality and the Law. London: Sage.

Information Commissioner (2001) The Data Protection Act 1998: Legal Guidance. Wilmslow: Information Commissioner.

Jenkins P (1997) Counselling, Psychotherapy and the Law. London: Sage.

Jenkins P (2001) Supervisory responsibility and the law. In Wheeler S, King D (eds) Supervising Counsellors: Issues of Responsibility. London: Sage.

Jenkins P (ed) (2002) Legal Issues in Counselling and Psychotherapy. London: Sage.

McGuire A (1997) False Memory Syndrome: a Statement Formally Adopted by the
    Management Committee. Rugby: BAC.
Stone J, Matthews J (1996) Complementary Medicine and the Law. Oxford: Oxford
    University Press.
Stone J (2002) An Ethical Framework for Complementary and Alternative Therapists.
    London: Routledge.
Walker M (2003) Abuse: Questions and Answers for Counsellors and Therapists.
    London: Whurr.

Insurance for therapists

H. and L. Balen & Co.
33 Graham Road
Great Malvern
Worcester WR14 2HU
(01684 893006)
(01684 893416 fax)

Psychologists' Protection Society
Standalane House
Kincardine
Alloa
Clackmannanshire FK10 4NX
(01259 730785)

Smithson Mason Ltd.
SMG House
31 Clarendon Road
Leeds LS2 9PA
(0113 294 4000)
(0113 294 4100 fax)

Official Organizations

Commission for Racial Equality
Elliott House
10-12 Allington Street
London SW1E 5EH
(020 7828 7022)
(020 7630 7605 fax)
website: www.cre.gov.uk

Commission for Racial Equality (Scotland)
The Tun
12 Jackson's Entry
Holyrood Road
Edinburgh EH8 8PJ
(0131 524 2000)
(0131 524 2001 fax)
email: scotland@cre.gov.uk

Commission for Racial Equality (Wales)
Third Floor
Capital Tower
Greyfriars Road
Cardiff CF1 3AG
(0290 729200)
(0290 729220 fax)
email: wales@cre.gov.uk

Criminal Injuries Compensation Board (northern United Kingdom)
Tay House
300 Bath Street
Glasgow G2 4LN
(0141 331 2287)

Criminal Injuries Compensation Board (southern United Kingdom)
Morley House
26-30 Holborn Viaduct
London EC1A 2JQ
(020 7482 6800)
website: www.cica.gov.uk

Crown Prosecution Service
50 Ludgate Hill
London
EC4M 7EX
(020 7796 8000)
website: www.cps.gov.uk

Disability Rights Commission
DRC Helpline
Freepost MID 02164
Stratford-upon-Avon
Warwickshire CV37 9HY
(08457 622633)
(08457 778878 fax)
(08457 622644 textphone)
email: Enquiry@drc-gb.org
website: www.drc-gb.org

Equal Opportunities Commission (Great Britain)
Arndale House
Arndale Centre
Manchester M4 3EQ
(0845 6015901)
(0161 838 1733 fax)
website: www.eoc.org.uk

Equal Opportunities Commission (Scotland)
St Stephens House
279 Bath Street
Glasgow G2 4JL
(0845 601 5901)
(0141 248 5834 fax)
website: scotland@eoc.org.uk

Equal Opportunities Commission (Wales)
Windsor House
Windsor Lane
Cardiff CF10 3GE
(029 2034 3552)
(029 2064 1079 fax)
website: wales@eoc.org.uk

Home Office
50 Queen Anne's Gate
London SW1H 9AT
(020 7273 4000)
website: www.homeoffice.gov.uk

Information Commissioner
Wycliffe House
Water Lane
Wilmslow
Cheshire SK9 5AF
(01625 545 745 enquiries)
(01625 535 711 administration)
website: www.dataprotection.gov.uk

Law Commission
Conquest House
37-38 John Street
Theobald's Road
London WC1N 2BQ
(020 7453 1220)
website: www.open.gov.uk/lawcomm

Law Society
113 Chancery Lane
London WC2A 1PL
(020 7242 1222)
website: www.lawsociety.org.uk

Legal Aid Board
85 Grays Inn Road
London WC1X 8TX
(020 7813 1000)
website: www.legalservices.gov.uk

Lord Chancellor's Department
Selbourne House
54-60 Victoria Street
London SW1E 6QW
(020 7210 0618)
(020 7210 0725 fax)
website: www.lcd.gov.uk

Mental Health Act Commission
Third Floor
Maid Marian House
56 Houndsgate
Nottingham NG1 6BG
(0115 943 7100)
website: www.mhac.trent.nhs.uk

Parliamentary and Health Service Ombudsman
Millbank Tower
Millbank
London SW1P 4QP
(0845 015 4033)
(020 7276 3000)
(020 7217 4163 fax)
website: www.ombudsman.org.uk

Secretary, European Commission of Human Rights
Council of Europe
F-67075 Strasbourg-Cedex
FRANCE
website: www.echr.coe.int

Therapists' organizations

British Association for Counselling and Psychotherapy
35-37 Albert Street
Rugby
Warwickshire CV21 2SG
(0870 443 5252)
website: www.bacp.co.uk

British Confederation of Psychotherapists
37a Mapesbury Road
London NW2 4HJ
(020 8830 5173)
website: www.bcp.org.uk

British Psychological Society
St Andrew's House
48 Princess Road East
Leicester LE1 7DR
(01162 549 568)
website: www.bps.org.uk

General Medical Council
44 Hallam Street
London W1N 6AE
(020 7580 7642)
website: www.gmc-uk.org

Independent Practitioners Network (IPNOSIS)
(address continues under next entry: The Alexander Group)

The Alexander Group
PO Box 19
Llandysul
Ceredigion SA44 4YE
(01545 560 402)
email: ipnosis@aol.com

Royal College of Psychiatrists
17 Belgrave Square
London SW1X 8PG
(020 7235 2351)
(020 7245 1231 fax)
website: www.rcpsych.ac.uk

United Kingdom Council for Psychotherapy
167-169 Great Portland Street
London W1W 5PF
(020 7436 3002)
website: www.ukcp.org.uk
website: www.psychotherapy.org.uk

Advocacy and consumer-support organizations

Academy of Experts
2 South Square
Grays Inn
London WC1R 5HP
(020 7637 0332)
(020 7637 1893 fax)
website: www.academy-experts.org.uk

Accuracy About Abuse
website: www.accuracyaboutabuse.org

Association of Child Abuse Lawyers
PO Box 466
Chorleywood
Rickmansworth
Hertfordshire
WD3 5LG
(01923 286 88)
website: www.childabuselawyers.com

Bar Pro Bono Unit
7 Grays Inn Square
London WC1R 5AZ
(020 7831 9733)
(020 7831 9711 fax)
website: www.probono.org.uk

British False Memory Society
Bradford-on-Avon
Wiltshire BA15 1N
(01225 868 682)
(01225 862 251 fax)
website: www.bfms.org.uk

Children's Legal Centre
University of Essex
Wivenhoe Park
Colchester
Essex CO4 3SQ
(01206 874416 office)
(01206-873820 advice Line)
website: www2.essex.ac.uk/clc

Citizen Advocacy Information and Training Alliance (CAIT)
162 Lee Valley Technopark
Ashley Road
London N17 9LN
(020 8880 4113)
email: cait@teleregion.co.uk

Consumers' Association (publishers of *Which?*)
2 Marylebone Road
London NW1 4DF
(020 7830 6000)
website: www.which.net

Free Representation Unit
49 Bedford Row
London WC1R 4LR
(0207 831 0692)

Freedom to Care (whistleblowers)
PO Box 125
West Molesey
Surrey KT8 1YE
(020 8224 1022)
email: freedomtocare@aol.com

Immunity Legal Centre (HIV+/AIDS)
First Floor
32-38 Osnaburgh Street
London NW1 3ND
(020 7388 6776)

Inquest (campaign on coroners' courts)
Ground Floor
Alexandra National House
330 Seven Sisters Road
Finsbury Park
London N4 2PJ
(020 8802 7430)
website: www.inquest.org.uk

Institute of Mental Health Law (training)
Murrayfield House
The King's Gap
Hoylake
Wirral L47 1HE
(0151 632 4115)
(0151 632 0090 fax)
website: www.imhl.com

Law Centres Federation
Duchess House
Warren Street
London W1P 5LR
(020 7387 8570)
website: www.lawcentres.org.uk

Legal Action Group
242-244 Pentonville Road
London N1 9UN
(020 7833 2931)
(020 7837 6094 fax)
website: www.lag.org.uk

MIND (National Association for Mental Health)
Granta House
15-19 Broadway
Stratford
London E15 4BQ
(020 8519 2122)
(020 8522 1725 fax)
(020 8522 1728 information line)
website: www.mind.org.uk

National Association of Citizens Advice Bureaux
Myddleton House
115-123 Pentonville Road
London N1 9LZ
website: www.nacab.org.uk

National Consumer Council
20 Grosvenor Gardens
London SW1 0DH
(020 7730 3469)
(020 7730 0191 fax)
website: www.ncc.org.uk

National Youth Advisory Service
1 Downham Road South
Heswall
Wirrall LT 60 5RG
(0151 342 7852)

POPAN (Prevention of Professional Abuse Network)
1 Wyvil Court
Wyvil Road
London SW8 2TG
(020 7622 6334)
(020 7622 9788 fax)
website: www.popan.org.uk

Public Concern at Work (whistleblowers)
Suite 306
16 Baldwin Gardens
London EC1N 7RJ
(020 7404 6609)
website: www.pcaw.org.uk

Public Law Project (support for judicial review procedures)
Birkbeck College
14 Bloomsbury Square
London WC1A 2LP
(020 7269 0570)
website: www.publiclawproject.org.uk

Refugee Legal Centre
153-157 Commercial Road
London E1 2DA
(020 7780 3200)
(020 7780 3201 fax)
website: www.refugee-legal-centre.org.uk

Rights of Women (legal advice on domestic violence)
52-54 Featherstone Street
London EC1Y 8RT
(020 7490 5377)
website: www.rightsofwomen.org.uk

Solicitors' Pro Bono Group
1 Pudding Lane
London EC3R 8AB
(0870 777 5601)
(020 7959 5722 fax)
website: www.probonogroup.org.uk

Stonewall (gay and lesbian rights)
46 Grosvenor Gardens
London SW1W 0EB
(020 7881 9440)
website: www.stonewall.org.uk

Survivors Speak Out (mental health survivors)
34 Osnaburgh Street
London NW1 3ND
(020 7916 5472)
(020 7916 5473 fax)
website: www.directions-plus.org.uk

Suzy Lamplugh Trust (protection at work)
14 East Sheen Avenue
London SW14 8AS
(0208 392 1839)
(020 8392 1830 fax)
website: www.suzylamplugh.org.uk

United Kingdom Advocacy Network (mental health survivors)
Suite 417
Premier House
14 Cross Burgess Street
Sheffield S1 2HG
(01142 753 131)
(web information via Citizen Advocacy Information and Training, see above)

VOICE (support in court for victims with learning disabilities)
Room B.11
College Business Centre
Uttoxeter New Road
Derby DE22 3WZ
(01332 202 555)
website: www.voiceuk.clara.net

Witness Support Programme
Victim Support
Cranmer House
39 Brixton Road
London SW9 6DZ
(020 7735 9166)
(020 7582 5712 fax)
website: www.victimsupport.org.uk

Complaints concerning legal representation

General Council of the Bar (barristers)
3 Bedford Row
London W1CR 4DB
(020 7242 0082)
website: www.barcouncil.org.uk

Legal Services Ombudsman
Third Floor
Sunlight House
Quay Street
Manchester M3 3JZ
(0161 839 7262)
(0161 832 5446 fax)
website: www.olso.org.uk

Office for the Supervision of Solicitors
Victoria Court
8 Dormer Place
Royal Leamington Spa
Warwickshire CV32 5AE
(01926 820 082)
(0845 608 6565)
website: www.lawsociety.org.uk

Mediation

Advisory, Conciliation and Arbitration Service
180 Borough High Street
London SE1 1LW
(020 7210 3613)
website: www.acas.org.uk

Centre for Effective Dispute Resolution
Exchange Tower
1 Harbour Exchange Square
London E14 9GB
(020 7536 6000)
website: www.cedr.co.uk

Divorce Conciliation and Advisory Service
38 Ebury Street
London SW1 0LU
(020 7730 2422)

Mediation UK (Alternative Dispute Resolution)
Alexander House
Telephone Avenue
Bristol BS1 4BS
(011 7904 6661)
(0117 904 3331 fax)
website: www.mediationuk.org.uk

National Family Mediation Charity Base
50 Westminster Bridge Road
London SE1 7QY
(020 7721 7658)

Family Mediators Association
Grove House
Grove Road
Bristol BS6 6UN
(0117 946 7180)
website: www.fmassoc.co.uk

The Cambridge Family and Divorce Centre
162 Tenison Road
Cambridge CB1 2DP
(01233 460136)

Legal references

Table of Cases (UK)

Table of Cases (US)

Table of Statutes (UK)

Index